THE INTERNET AS A GAME

ELECTRACY AND TRANSMEDIA STUDIES
Series Editors: Jan Rune Holmevik and Cynthia Haynes

The Electracy and Transmedia Studies Series publishes research that examines the mixed realities that emerge through electracy, play, rhetorical knowledge, game design, community, code, and transmedia artifacts. This book series aims to augment traditional artistic and literate forms with examinations of electrate and literate play in the age of transmedia. Writing about play should, in other words, be grounded in playing with writing. The distinction between play and reflection, as Stuart Moulthrop argues, is a false dichotomy. Cultural transmedia artifacts that are interactive, that move, that are situated in real time, call for inventive/electrate means of creating new scholarly traction in transdisciplinary fields. The series publishes research that produces such traction through innovative processes that move research forward across its own limiting surfaces (surfaces that create static friction). The series exemplifies extreme points of contact where increased electrate traction might occur. The series also aims to broaden how scholarly treatments of electracy and transmedia can include both academic and general audiences in an effort to create points of contact between a wide range of readers. The Electracy and Transmedia Series follows what Gregory Ulmer calls an image logic based upon a wide scope— "an aesthetic embodiment of one's attunement with the world."

BOOKS IN THE SERIES

The Internet as a Game by Jill Anne Morris (2018)
Identity and Collaboration in World of Warcraft by Phillip Michael Alexander (2018)
Future Texts: Subversive Performance and Feminist Bodies, edited by Vicki Callahan and Virginia Kuhn (2016)
Play/Write: Digital Rhetoric, Writing, Games, edited by Douglas Eyman and Andréa D. Davis (2016)

SITES

Gregory Ulmer's *Konsult Experiment*: http://konsultexperiment.com/

THE INTERNET AS A GAME

Jill Anne Morris

Parlor Press
Anderson, South Carolina
www.parlorpress.com

Parlor Press LLC, Anderson, South Carolina, USA
© 2018 by Parlor Press
All rights reserved.
Printed in the United States of America on acid-free paper.

S A N: 2 5 4 - 8 8 7 9

Library of Congress Cataloging-in-Publication Data on File

978-1-64317-024-4 (paperback)
978-1-64317-025-1 (hardcover)
978-1-64317-026-8 (pdf)
978-1-64317-027-5 (ePub)

1 2 3 4 5

Electracy and Transmedia Studies
Series Editors: Jan Rune Holmevik and Cynthia Haynes

Cover image: Photo by sebastiaan stam on Unsplash. Used by permission. https://unsplash.com/photos/KuMHZq-o6Zw
Copyeditor: Jared Jameson.
Cover design: David Blakesley

Parlor Press, LLC is an independent publisher of scholarly and trade titles in print and multimedia formats. This book is available in paper, cloth and eBook formats from Parlor Press on the World Wide Web at http://www. parlorpress.com or through online and brick-and-mortar bookstores. For submission information or to find out about Parlor Press publications, write to Parlor Press, 3015 Brackenberry Drive, Anderson, South Carolina, 29621, or email editor@parlorpress.com.

Contents

Acknowledgments

I am most thankful to Cynthia Haynes and Jan Rune Holmevik for their continued support, and to my dogs—Delilah and Riddle—who had to stay awake with me over the nights that I decided to write instead of sleep.

Preface: Utopia vs. Trolls

The truth is that in the beginning everyone thought that the Internet was going to be theirs—it didn't matter if you were a feminist or a revolutionary in a war-torn country or a teacher or a conservative extremist, a new online world without rules or borders could be used to unite everyone who you thought was worth uniting. The story can be told in a million ways, even though eventually some of those stories proved to be false. This "brave new world" was going to change everything for the better, but the betters that were imagined were incredibly different. One story might go like this:

Once upon a time, in an Internet far, far away (so about the year 2001 or so), feminists and other socially liberal groups dreamed of a utopian digital space where radical concepts could be discussed and disseminated and where personal experiences could be made political and shared amongst a network of like-minded individuals easily and quickly. Women whose personal experiences led them to feminism (rather than their academic sensibilities, though that still happened too) could share those stories, and thus feminist rhetoric and theory could be created and recreated, crowd-sourced, shared, and argued about at length. Women would be cyborgs, and cyborgs would lead the technological revolution.

But that story—like all the others—came at a price. For now, no one owns what we used to call "cyberspace," and the price we pay has become trolling, harassment, and even simply hate. We dreamed of a homogenous utopia, rather than a diverse one, and as a result we are still entrenched in a cultural war about what that utopia is meant to homogenize into.[*]

Any number of books about the early Internet are sure to mention "cyberfeminism" as an influential sphere in online practices of the late 1990s and early 2000s. Commercials of the 1990s had promised this

---

[*] Content warning: This text contains direct quotes and discussion of online posts, emails, private messages, and other communication that may contain racism, misogyny, homophobia, transphobia, or other hate speech. Theory is presented outside of these examples and may be read on its own at the reader's discretion.

space without gender, race, or class, and we largely embraced (if not believed) that the "Internet Superhighway" would change the way we interacted with one another forever. If we were not involved in social justice (as I was not at that time), we thought that the Internet was going to connect us to people from all over the world, and that we were going to have friends from all other countries and be able to talk to them either through translation software or by learning each other's languages.

Today I show the "Internet Superhighway" (Network MCI, 1994) commercial to my students and they ask questions like, "Did anyone really ever believe this?" I think to myself: of course we did. It was easy to be short-sighted if you stayed around safe communities. It was even easier to give in to the fantasy—television shows predicted an embodied internet full of avatars that were raceless, classless, and genderless and online text-based games at the time had twenty-seven potential genders. Of course, it didn't take long for even "safe" communities to find their detractors. For a while, during the time when I was an undergraduate, I ran the "World's Largest *Fraggle Rock* Website," (Henson, 1983–1987) and from that site I met my first troll. He was younger than me, claimed that he was remaking the *Fraggle Rock* puppets in his garage, and he stole tons of the material that I had personally spent hours digitizing. He sent me harassing emails, contacted my University (since I was running the site off a server in my dorm room), and would find me online at other sites to attack anything and everything I posted. Eventually I moved out of the dorms and the site was consequently shut down—no doubt he took credit.

Not long after, I began to discover that any time I tried to take a position online on discussion boards and comment sections that wasn't black/white or yes/no that I was accused of nihilism, ignored, or made fun of. I wanted to find out why. It had become clear to me that there had been trouble in paradise nearly as long as paradise has existed no matter what the theory and commercials were telling me. I sat in classes where we learned about using technologies in classrooms and how to use them with our students, and I couldn't help but think that the students were probably experiencing the same things that I was—and they weren't as happy about classroom technology use as they told their teachers they were. Though I loved teaching students to code and do graphic design alongside how to write, there was something off-putting about the communities that we ran and worked within—they didn't look like other online communities, some of the lessons learned in class didn't carry over onto the Internet at large, and it all felt a little bit dishonest.

In the spring of 2006, I was a PhD student and had been studying technofeminist blogs for a class project. One of my sites of study was the "Den of the Biting Beaver," a feminist blog written by "BB." BB's experiences were drastically different from my own, but despite holding feminist ideals far more radical than mine, I found her writing to usually be engaging. She narratively described the path she took to feminism, and it was one rife with abuse but always also entertaining, at times positive, and I looked forward to her updates despite not always agreeing with her. However, that spring a number of feminist blogs nearly simultaneously came under attack from a group of highly organized trolls. They not only made fun of her but also threatened to rape her, told her that she was not properly serving her husband, wanted her to allow her son to look at porn, and wanted to expose her and everyone that posted on her site for their "radical" beliefs in women's general equality (which they, of course, said really meant superiority to and hatred of men). There were certainly plenty of radical elements to her site, but she was a decent writer for a blogger at that time, and even if I wasn't as radical I was drawn into the community that supported her. She rigidly deleted off-topic comments on her site to keep it "safe" for other users.

BB came out against the trolls, not surprisingly, claiming her site was a safe space for radical feminists. There were many feminist sites online, but most of them were made for people like me who came to feminism from relatively "cushy" positions and who were more accepting of a wider range of feminisms. Radical feminism, at the time, didn't have the same sort of support network that it would develop ten years later on Tumblr and other similar sites (though hatred of "Tumblr Feminism" and "Social Justice Warriors" is a problem as of 2014–15, and the culture that has developed from it is also seen as problematic by some feminists). At that time, BB wrote: "This space has been and always will be, a space intended to give voice and courage to those women who have neither, and I will not allow that to be compromised" (BB, 1 January 2006). However, she was not able to prevail. Within a year her site was made private as she could no longer stand against the rising tide of hatred and vitriol directed at her.

The trolls worked together. There were hundreds of them. They all threatened the same things—rape, mostly, but also removal of her teenage son from her home because she was "ruining him." They posted her real name ("doxxing"—a practice that also sometimes includes home address, phone numbers, and workplace) to a centralized website. Before the trolls she had lamented that her teenage son (named Brandon) would not stop looking at porn and she feared that his attachment to porn and showing it to his little brother could one day lead him to become a rapist or misogynist himself. The trolls believed that her son had a right to see porn, and that BB had no right to prevent him. Because she was teaching him about feminism and wanted him to stay away from porn they sought to "free" him from her "tyranny." Since the son was not located, it is hard to say what he felt about his mom's teachings, but they assumed that he would be psychologically scarred by them. In addition, the right to view materials like porn online is often equated with calls for free speech by groups of trolls.

Their attacks were personal, but not exactly rhetorical. They primarily focused upon BB's character—throwing *ad hominem* and *ad baculum* at her in particularly vicious ways. In traditional rhetoric, of course, these are fallacies and, therefore, not effective. In response, she posted feminist theory, guarding herself with traditional rhetoric. But it didn't work. As many people know (myself included) and have personally experienced—arguing online using traditional rhetorical methods is rarely effective. The rhetorical tools we build in classrooms, journals, and other academic spaces were laughed at in the networked space that BB had built for herself even though it was her space. Fallacies were far more effective, even if they were so by invoking fear.

BB came across as increasingly paranoid, believing herself to be under attack from a larger group. Today, more people have heard about the large groups of organized individuals that can descend upon practically anyone online that posts a dissenting opinion. At that time, suggesting that harassers are organized sounded like a conspiracy theory. However, when her children began to receive threats as well, she finally removed herself from "the blogosphere" altogether. She received little support from the larger online community, possibly because she believed that there was an organization conspiring against her. The problem is—she was kind of right.

Names of vaguely familiar websites—4Chan, Anonymous, Party-Van—kept showing up in the deleted comments and e-mails that she was receiving. In 2007 these were not yet in the news. I had asked her for access to her deleted comments—she sent me two hundred pages of deleted e-mails and comments. By this time, I was deeply invested in research for that aforementioned class about why rhetorical arguments in networked systems fail so often. I had several hypotheses—none of them were supported by the attacks that she had received. I visited 4Chan but because the site has very little archival material and isn't very searchable I was not able to trace messages back to it. One night, I searched for the PartyVan—and discovered the link that both BB and I had been missing.

What would your reaction be to stumbling upon a page where a group of anonymous individuals are able to plan and carry out harassment on people and groups? These plans include directions about how to incapacitate website servers, how and where to post in response to these groups or individuals, and that seemed to carry no respect for the people being targeted in the least. Welcome to what was (once) the PartyVan Wiki—the organizational tool for a group of vigilantes and hackers known online simply as "Anonymous." Would you be frightened? Confused? Angry? Excited? It depends on who is being attacked by those tools. It can be shocking and scary if you see information about attacking people that you can imagine as colleagues or friends. It can be exciting if you see ways to destroy people you would consider your enemies.

The original directions for how she was to be harassed (which was a live, ongoing "raid" at the time, their terminology borrowing language from MMORPGs) are no longer posted online. However, there is a document still describing the "Feminazi" war, and she is a listed target on the site to this day.

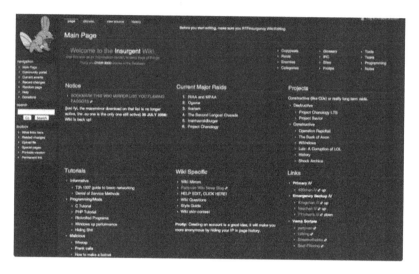

Figure 1. PartyVan Wiki Main Page. Screenshot by the author.

The PartyVan Wiki described the actions of BB's harassers as heroic—as if they were going into battle. For example, they write:

> Anonymous first engaged the feminazis in glorious battle when a post made by BitingBeaver circa July 2007 gained wide notoriety across the internets. When her son Brandon hit puberty, BitingBeaver was disgusted to discover that a lifetime of feminist indoctrination was no match for his libido, as Brandon had no qualms about looking for porn online. BitingBeaver claims that Brandon was the product of marital rape and expressed regrets that she didn't abort him. This angered Anonymous to no end. (PartyVan Wiki, 2013)

Under this description was a list of methods used to harass and threaten her. Upon first viewing I immediately spotted some of the very same quotes I had seen repeated over and over again in her deleted e-mails.

While originally setting out to try to explain and describe general flames and attacks in rhetorical terms, I began searching for a way to describe these particular sorts of attacks. They were planned. They were carried out by hundreds—if not thousands—of people at once. They had rules. They were full of memes. "Jokes" were repeated again and again.

More interestingly, many of the people that made these threats and attacks claimed in other comments to not even believe in what they were saying. They were aware that they were following the pack and doing what they were told—but as a member of the group that called itself "Anonymous" at that moment they did not care. It was "fun" or "something to do." Some of them even attempted to tell her how to get them to stop.

I set out then to find an explanation or metaphor for what happened on the PartyVan Wiki and during the attacks they carried out. During the study that followed (four years of online ethnographic research followed by two years of less intense research during times of activity), I watched Anonymous change from a group primarily focused on individuals like BB to one that carried out worldwide attacks on the Church of Scientology, the KKK, and ISIS. Later they would mobilize to try to find the Boston Marathon bombers and other criminals, and even take a stand against President Donald Trump. While finding some criminals (generally those wanted for child porn) was always part of their planning site, looking for criminals and seeking justice has become far more important to them than attacking feminists or other minority groups or even obnoxious people online. When Gamergate occurred (another attack featuring some of the same types of characters that will be discussed in detail in later chapters), Anonymous even stood up to the gamers organizing against feminists and video game journalists alike—a complete reversal in focus. When some members of the attacks on BB seemed to tell her that it wasn't about *her* per se, but instead they would attack whomever they were told, they might have been right. One user said, "We don't hate feminists, we might be attacking MRAs next week" (MRAs are Men's Right's Activists). However, as time has passed, the development of the Alt-Right, which uses some of the same rhetorical techniques online, suggests that while it is impossible to tell if trolls or members of anonymous groups actually agree with the group, it may be dangerous to take their postings just "in fun"—as I may have suggested years ago. Even when used to expose powerful men of sexual assault, the internet tools described within such as "doxxing" can be used by *anyone*, and we must decide all over again whether we really want a society where anyone can hold the social and rhetorical power to convince others and potentially harm someone's life outside of our legal system. Is doxxing a new form of sophistry? Or do we need new terms to describe this sort of rhetoric, leaving the sophists untouched?

Having identified patterns in these original attacks against BB, I found many more sites of study (which are described in the cases in the chapters that follow). But one truth emerged—nobody knows what to do when hundreds, if not thousands, of people swarm your site online. Feminists, lone individuals, the Church of Scientology, and even large organizations like the RIAA have little to no recourse in the face of massive-scale planned attacks. Traditional rhetoric fails in the face of these attacks. BB was not the first nor last individual to shut down her website and hide her online presence because of 4Chan, Anonymous, or other groups like them, and without understanding how and why the rhetoric of these groups work, few organizations or individuals would be able to resist. (And indeed, one must ask if we even should teach resistance—a liberally minded person might want to see feminist websites survive, but what about websites ran by white supremacists?)

4Chan and Anonymous have transformed in the time since the studies that were the foundation for this theory began. In 2007, 4Chan (especially one specific board within called /b/) was primarily a random imageboard that hosted lots of memes and trolling. On one hand, the anonymity of all posters meant that rapid-fire development of popular new media and memes was and is occurring—if you ever thought a picture was funny online, it probably started on 4Chan. On the other hand, members treated one another poorly on purpose and trolled one another, and often went on "raids" wherein they organized and would troll another site. They might, for example, post lots of pictures of dogs on cat sites, though most raids are not what would be considered innocuous.

Anonymous is a group that grew out of 4Chan; the name is a result of people posting there being referred to as "anons" for their anonymous nature. The term and group has taken on a life of its own and began using trolling for more serious purposes as well, such as trying to shut down the Church of Scientology, protesting ISIS, finding animal abusers, and attempting to get rape cases investigated. They still loosely organize around IRC rooms and Facebook, but have largely left their PartyVan wiki.

I even found that it was impossible to read a lot of the trolls' rhetoric without starting to find it funny. No, I didn't start to find racist jokes funny—but there was a biting humor to a lot of what they posted online. Some of what has occurred since the early days of trolling's emergence as a subculture is impossible to ignore as downright humorous—a thread on 4Chan about the new *My Little Pony* (Faust, 2010) incarnation in 2010, for example, came out as against an article that claimed the series was nothing but an attempt to make money from toys. Those initial trolls claimed the show was awesome—and then they watched it, and we can assume that at least some of them found it awesome. They created a "mods are asleep, post ponies" meme, people started creating lots of fan works related to the ponies, and the Brony (adult, male My Little Pony fan) movement was born. It now features a convention that attracts thousands each year. The irreverent humor of trolls can be very catchy, and it is one that our students are well-versed in.

I believe that all individuals online (and especially students) can benefit by learning to read online conversations and arguments in new ways. In fact, I think it may be our duty to do so. We must understand when we are being influenced by group rhetoric or swayed by protocols or procedural rhetoric. By understanding and even using some of the techniques of the oppressors and trolls in this story and those to follow, digital rhetoricians can be far more effective in their persuasive efforts and learn to recognize patterns and procedures in arguments as just those—patterns and procedures. These procedures are game-like and playful as well as sometimes awful and hateful. By taking the good of these methods we can build a procedural rhetoric of online conversations, and we can build a rhetoric of online argument from gaming into reality. This rhetoric is playful and procedural and can be employed by many people at once to great (or terrible) ends. We cannot forget, however, that trolls are not a single anonymous entity—they exist on both the left and the right and are not as apolitical as they once avowed. Anonymous group rhetoric can both support and destroy fascism—but only if we are willing to study it.

1 Introduction: The Internet as a Game

Ever get the feeling you're playing some vast and useless game whose goal you don't know and whose rules you can't remember? Ever get the fierce desire to quit, to resign, to forfeit, only to discover there's no umpire, no referee, no regulator to whom you can announce your capitulation? Ever get the vague dread that while you have no choice but to play the game, you can't win it, can't know the score, or who keeps it? Ever suspect that you don't even know who your real opponent might be? Ever get mad over the obvious fact that the dice are loaded, the deck stacked, the table rigged and the fix—in? Welcome to gamespace.

—McKenzie Wark, 2007

Throughout this text I pose one question: what if the rhetoric of video games could be made useful in systems outside of the immediate realm of video games? Through defining some digital communications practices as game-like, I will show how looking at other online and digital rhetorics—specifically online arguments in unmoderated and anonymous communities—as games can be fruitful exercises for explaining the way these rhetorics work procedurally and identifying how respondents can regain power within them. While other writers in gaming studies have described the interaction of game and narrative, the effects of avatar on identity, using games as persuasion, using serious games to teach, and how games and play can benefit pedagogy, none of these types of studies begins to use the discoveries of gaming studies in other rhetorical situations. Applying procedural rhetoric outside of games proper can be a fruitful process used to analyze communication wherein traditional rhetoric fails.

As demonstrated by McKenzie Wark in *Gamer Theory* (2007), it is possible to argue that our culture is dominated by gaming already (i.e., we are always already in a game—already enmeshed in a metaphor of gaming). We are surrounded by language wherein winning is important—whether that be at school, work, or play. It is nearly impossible to escape competition of one sort or another. In many digital networks this is certainly true. Unless rigidly monitored, controlled, or moderated, Internet spaces can become highly competitive and even (textually) violent no matter what topic the original conversation was about. While one of the rules of the Internet states that if something exists, there is also porn of it, there might as well be a rule that if something exists, somebody cares enough to get into a fight about it. Networked systems are especially liable to be co-opted for gaming because of their nature, design, and history. While the Internet cannot be *called* a game because not everyone involved is actively playing or thinking of it as such, nor does everyone using it visit communities where game-like arguments happen, viewing Internet arguments through the lens of gaming allows analysis of arguments that are not otherwise considered to be rhetorical and therefore is a potentially useful practice.

Many—if not most—Internet arguments stray into *ad baculum* and *ad hominem* attacks, relying upon what would ordinarily be considered logical fallacies to silence respondents and "win" arguments. Because of this, they are study-able only in limited rhetorical context. At the same time, these attacks are highly effective. The story of Biting Beaver (shared in the Preface) is just one of thousands (and more) of examples of historically disenfranchised people like women, people of color, LGTB groups, children, and others that lose their voice online because of more powerful groups using game-like strategies to silence them. This is truer than ever with the rise of the Alt-Right and extreme conservative groups that have coopted the voice of trolling as their own. While the targeted groups might seem to be being chosen because of their status in larger society, trolls often report that it is the *rhetorical strategies* of their targets that leave them vulnerable. It wasn't what was communicated that drew an attack—it was the way it was communicated. (This does *not* apply to the 2014 attacks on ISIS—in that case the message is far more important than the medium.)

Disenfranchised groups often use traditional rhetoric in their websites, message boards, and other online communication. It is outside the realm of this study to determine why this is exactly; however, *tone* is often discussed in meta-argumentation. Women do not want to sound "shrill" or "uppity" should they fail to restrain themselves to polite language and phrasing, for example, as they have been taught to be more conciliatory. In other cases, perhaps these groups feel as though using both Standard American English (SAE) and traditional rhetoric strengthens their argument because we are *all* taught in United States' schools and universities that these are more or less required for clarity and to reach a wide audience. Using SAE also allows disenfranchised groups to "pass" as rhetorically un-othered, even as those in the majority propagate the use of memes, misspellings, and language shortcuts only meaningful in digital systems (for example: the use of "because *noun/adjective*," a currently popular phrase used in situations such as describing why someone has handed in a paper late as "because lazy," grammatically incorrect but meaningful online).

But traditional arguments and even formal language usage fail more often than not when we are fighting against a group in a digital space—especially over controversial topics. They attract trolls who are looking for anyone that is taking online space too seriously. We are taught things like "don't feed the trolls" when people are intentionally caustic online. If you ignore them, the common parlance states, they will go away. Don't let them see you sweat. Don't let them get a rise out of you. However, this treatment means that some sites are eventually abandoned (when existing at all means "feeding the trolls"), it means that we learn nothing from the argumentation methods that are used by powerful online groups, and it means that all hope of education and learning through dialectic is lost. Also—let's face it—sometimes it works just about as well as ignoring a bully on the playground did when you were in fourth grade. Past studies of trolls, flame wars, and other rhetorical issues online seemed to suggest that this is part of online life and is not changeable (Dery, 1994). While anonymity can breed experimentation with hate, it is not necessary to purely accept this hate as ultimately unrhetorical, nor is it necessary to reject funny, clever, but not-traditional communication as un-analyzable or unteachable.

Gaming is a potentially useful lens for these types of arguments because, as Ian Bogost notes in *Persuasive Games* (2007), video games are procedural—they communicate through a series of steps (procedures) using code and by following rule-based symbolic manipulations. As I discovered in investigating why BB was attacked in the way that she was, many arguments taken on by large groups online are procedural. People participating are given lists of potential arguments to make, names to call the site owner or others they disagree with, addresses to harass, and so on. Participants use their knowledge of memes, as well, to speed up the process of communication. Trolling is very procedural, especially when it is planned on a wiki or in an IRC space. To make it easy for many people to form a community (which I will define as an *ad-hoc* in chapter 2), these procedures are shared explicitly or implicitly with all participants. While these initial procedures may seem juvenile (*ad hominem* attacks, DDoS attacks on servers, or hundreds of pizzas sent to an address, for example), the development of channels of shared procedural rhetoric have also allowed these same communities to mobilize thousands of members to protest injustices in the Church of Scientology, expose elicit government practices, find terrorists, and stop animal abuse. These same practices could be used in other circles online for rhetorical purposes if properly contextualized. Furthermore, as has been written about by Whitney Phillips (2015), trolls have a reciprocal relationship with the media, have greatly influenced online culture, and are—at times—both persuasive and funny. They deserve greater attention and so does their rhetoric.

This book, then, examines using gaming studies as a lens for online rhetoric. Viewing the Internet and other digital rhetorics through the lens of gaming is a beneficial rhetorical exercise that enables us to identify textual, visual, and multimedia arguments as possessing uniquely ludic rhetorical tropes to better understand and teach best practices. If we do, what additional conservations, arguments, images, and creative works could be seen as rhetorical and analyzable that were previously not? If we agree that procedural rhetoric exists in some online communities as a means of persuasion, does strict moderation or none at all lead to more procedural rhetoric? Stated rules or implied rules? Few rules or many rules? Should we encourage the use of procedural rhetoric outside of software and video games? If so, how should procedural rhetorics that are not tied to games or software be taught? Which should our students be analyzing and learning to reproduce? Lastly, what is the place of written, visual, multimedia, and multimodal rhetoric in such procedural rhetorics?

Literature Review

The Internet was often described in literature and ads from the 1990s and 2000s as a utopian world devoid of race, utterly genderless, and without boundaries between class or country (Turkle, 1997; Selfe,

1991; Stone, 1995; Poster, 2006). Because people are "invisible" and anonymous online, earlier theoreticians and even advertisers expected that virtual networks would draw people closer to one another and allow us to see our similarities when our differences were hidden. That, sadly, has not been the case. While the Internet has certainly opened access to a large amount of information most users did not have access to before, it has not erased hate or discrimination and is more often a site of incensed argumentation between people of different genders, races, classes, and even countries than one that "brings us together." Insistence upon free speech supports hate just as easily as social justice.

Scholarship in computers and composition has generally focused on online identity, technological determinism, new media rhetoric, pedagogy, video games in classrooms, and so on. As a field, we have a great deal of enthusiasm for using new tools for research, writing, and collaboration in our classrooms, and the past thirty years have seen those tools transform the inside of writing classrooms in all types of schools. But more often than not we are using these new tools to teach old rhetorics—even though teaching ethos/logos/pathos using YouTube, websites, and music is effective, flashy, and keeps students' attention, for example, those terms can be just as well taught with books, handouts, and overhead projectors. Students, of course, can also *create* new media as part of writing classes (and my own students certainly do—they make movies, animations, websites, book chapters, posters, video games, and even program robots just for a few examples), but again they are asked to do so in service of the same style of argumentation we have always taught. It is only in recent years after performing the research in this book that even I have begun to encourage non-traditional rhetoric that looks more like other argumentation online in these projects (see chapter 6 for examples). Stereotypically, even though some digital rhetorics turn the rhetorical triangle into a rhetorical tesseract, students are usually taught methods of rhetorical persuasion through those tools best suited to writing or art (in the case of visual rhetoric), and less suited to the networked communication that we use to spruce up our own classrooms.

I simply don't think that studying digital forms in these ways prepares students for the rhetorical situations they face online. When your online audience is likely to say things like "all your carefully constructed arguments will be ignored and used against you," it is easy to imagine that teaching them to construct carefully crafted traditional arguments on digital systems might seem dishonest. Traditional rhetoric (even in digital writing) has a place still, of course, but in online communities it is typically ineffective. Online users do not just want to be able to read and process arguments quickly because they are lazy and have short attention spans (Barnes, Marateo, & Ferris, 2007), but instead because community standards have normalized the "tl;dr." *Tl;dr* stands for "too long; didn't read," and is often put at the end of a longer post or blog entry with a brief, one-sentence-or-less restatement of the key points (better still, they'd like you to make it into a video). While it might be easy to see the tl;dr as a sign of our impending rhetorical doom and a failure of education to produce individuals that are capable of reading extended arguments, creating a short, pithy, and at times witty summary of an argument could be seen as an excellent rhetorical exercise in thesis creation—much as Twitter can be. If a single image (or series of images that has become a meme) can be just as persuasive as a book, why wouldn't someone want to just look at the image? Furthermore, digital spaces create blurred lines between types of rhetoric—the digital leaking into the procedural into the visual and even the traditional—and can be taught and studied as such.

Much more importantly to myself, students' past experiences with Internet communication color their willingness to write the same in classrooms. If they already know feminist arguments are often rejected online and attract trolls, they certainly aren't going to respond favorably in a public course blog when asked about feminism. They might even resist by refusing to make the posts or engage with the material. Other students come to college with pre-conceived notions that they themselves do not belong online, and for a variety of reasons that extend far beyond "I'm bad at computers."

GENDER AND RACE ONLINE

In 2006, I was teaching a freshman composition course at Wayne State University. Wayne State is in downtown Detroit, and many of our students were people of color. I was encouraging students to post to the course blog, and one student in the back of the room raised his hand. I smiled and called on him—he always had something interesting to say. That day the interesting thing was "Look, if you put this on Blackboard or make it private we'll write. But the Internet is for white people." Other students nodded.

It is a moment that has stuck with me, though I have not found anyone else that is willing to say it so bluntly. Online posts about gender or race are often met with derision in the online communities I study. Racists have found the Internet just as readily as people of color and their allies. Other people simply think that it is funny to say the worst possible thing to make others angry—and often enough that "thing" is racist in nature. Still others have co-opted the language of trolling to spread white supremacy. Teaching my students traditional digital rhetoric was not giving them tools to defend themselves online or make them feel like online even *belonged* to them. Asking them to post online about race and gender is also painting giant targets on their work—no matter how safe the learning environment is in my classroom, I cannot create that same safe space in the Internet at large. In some cases, maybe I wouldn't even want to, but it's hard to ask people to experiment in a space they don't feel safe in, especially if they feel like the sorts of media they are posting won't be well-received.

In many cases, "political" conversations about gender and race aren't even allowed in some communities to keep the peace. As early as 2000, Beth Kolko (with Nakamura and Rodman) wrote that race and gender are mostly invisible online, and conversations about them in some communities are not allowed or are likely to cause "flame wars" (heated conversations that quickly turn from civilized discourse into personal attacks and hate). At that time many individuals "passed" as white and male online simply by not stating their own gender or race. Since 2000, companies like Facebook have made it more popular to not be completely anonymous online—we use Facebook to comment on political articles on some news sites, for example—which means that race is more visible than it used to be. Even so, discussing issues of race and gender are still likely to cause problems and some communities still outlaw such discussions. If you cannot discuss your own lived experience in context online, feeling unwelcome in that space is far from unreasonable.

In the 1990s and early 2000s, "safe spaces" for people of color, women, LGTBQ individuals, and others became popular. I will not argue against the need for spaces where marginalized groups can feel safe, where they can discuss issues without having to teach allies, and where they can share resources—such spaces, online and off, are invaluable. However, arguments made within those spaces—no matter how eloquent—also fail at persuading the larger populace because it is not the point of their existence. While this protects their creators, writing only for those that listen to you is unlikely to create long term change in online practices or the world at large. I don't just wish to teach students to write arguments that persuade those that agree with them online—I want to teach them to change public opinion and have their voice heard outside of my classroom, their own circle of friends, or their colleagues.

HATE AND FLAME WARS

Online hate, flame wars, and trolling have all been studied, of course, as has hate speech outside of networked communication. Studies not specifically related to hate speech tend to reduce these communicative acts as being a-rhetorical (it's not rhetoric if you harm or threaten to harm another person). But easily dismissing flame wars and trolls as being unpersuasive misses the very real effects they have on victim's lives and just how they function to silence vulnerable populations online. It also completely misses that trolls themselves identify highly with Plato's Socrates and even consider him the very first troll (Phillips, 2015). Some also study closely the work of Arthur Schopenhauer (2013) to get a better reaction out of their intended online targets and to hone their rhetorical craft. Schopenhauer is, of course, sarcastic in much of his writing—but so are the trolls that follow him. While it is probably not fair to say that everyone who calls him or herself a rhetorician is one, actively studying rhetoric and making use of what they learn in embedded contexts is probably closer to being a rhetorician than much work students perform in school.

Some studies have focused in varying ways on how companies, businesses, and other entities can respond to online threats without considering how individuals might learn to deflect, respond, or even persuade using similar (but non-incendiary) procedures themselves. For example, in *Virtual Justice* Lastowka (2010) discusses how the Internet has become a space that challenges traditional laws and jurisprudence. Instead of focusing on how power and rhetoric functions within communities, however, he focuses instead on how governments and NGOs have responded to online threats, privacy, rights, and property. Although he touches on decentralized architecture and the communities it has helped build, his ultimate focus is on the national and international governmental response to those architectures—

not on the rhetoric that the communities have created or the ways power works from within the communities instead of from without. In other words, rather than focusing on *how* communities have created their own rhetorics and power structures he considers how traditional power structures might respond. Similarly, other texts such as *Games of Empire* (2009) study the connection between Hardt and Negri's *Empire* (2001) and show how games demonstrate cultural, political, and economic forces of global capital. Other texts expose the idea that a truly free digital space online never existed, such as *The Myth of Digital Democracy*, showing that being able to talk is not the same as having a voice (Hindman, 2008).

AD BACULUM AND AD HOMINEM

Douglas Walton has written several texts specifically on *ad baculum* and *ad hominem*, the most important of which are *The Place of Emotion in Argument* (1992) and *Ad Hominem Arguments* (1998). Fallacies are important to this discussion because if personal attacks and threats weren't fallacies we would be able to look at them as rhetorical (and not just procedurally). He defines *ad baculum* in these texts as any time that fear is used, not just when a threat is made. The traditional *ad baculum* that will be seen repeatedly in the conversations I analyze later is a threat. But according to Walton, an insurance advertisement (for example) that tries to make people afraid of their house burning down is just as much an *ad baculum* attack as a death threat on the Internet. This wide definition allows him to make many interesting arguments about attack-based speech, but not all are applicable to the cases I study here. *Of course* threats are effective—if they were not they would not be so popular. But how can ordinary citizens defend themselves, educate others about whatever they wish to argue about and for, and continue to post online in relative safety?

As for the second *ad* I shall focus on, the framework he identifies for showing that *ad hominem* attacks are not always fallacious has been of use in developing schemes and protocols for the online communities that I study in this text (Walton, 1998). However, Walton himself never studied online communities, in part due to when his book was published, which limits the usability of his text in online environments. He also believes that while appeals to emotion and even threats can be used legitimately, we must be careful that they are not used fallaciously (whereas in later chapters I will show that fallacious speech can have procedural rhetorical value even if it does not have traditionally rhetorical value). Whately (1836) believed that arguments otherwise called *fallacious* are only fallacies when used unfairly. If an Internet argument is being viewed as a game, then the only unfair argument is that which is against the rules—and in many of the spaces I will discuss such arguments are not against the rules. They do tend to hide their own weakness behind emotion and fear, but this also makes them exploitable.

Walton also limits emotional arguments considered "good" as those that allow us to "link an argument to an arguer's so-called dark side commitments on an issue" (1992, p. 27), which not only belies the fact this book was written in the time of *Star Wars* (the first edition was published in 1986), but minimizes the impact of the argument of the attack on the victim. Despite this, his work does point to the potential for context to change a fallacious argument into a non-fallacious one, with the example that appealing to force is perfectly appropriate in negotiation-speech.

Online Communities: More Is Different

Networked communities often have languages, rules, and beliefs built into their history and culture that makes it difficult for them to talk with one another without conflict. We are used to being constrained by topic and opinion, so being in the same community as people with grossly differing opinions can be affronting. Mark Poster (2006) believes that networks allow cultural exchange (a good thing) that indirectly leads to groups online that are incapable of decoding each other's messages as being politically un-noxious (a bad thing). He says that culture should be interpreted as "multiple cacophonies of inscribed meanings as each cultural object moves across cultural differences" (2006, p. 11). Such cultural exchanges lead us to be accountable to one another. If we fail to exchange cultural objects (such as memes and jokes), then communities cannot communicate, play, and have fun with one another. Technology itself does not automatically create a neutral or politically ethical environment, though exchanges of play between communities could be a good first step.

Trolling is, in part, so difficult to understand from the outside because it has developed its own language that only other trolls (and those who interact with them) understand. Trolls make as much use of that language as possible in order to hide in plain sight. My favorite example occurred when Oprah Winfrey had been lobbying against online sexual predators. A troll visited her message board and posted a brief piece of text that would be immediately recognized by other trolls as part of their lexicon. That would have been nearly immediately forgotten, except that Oprah announced, live on air, "let me read you something from my message board, from somebody who claims to be a member of a known pedophile network: He said he does not forgive. He does not forget. His group has over 9000 penises and they're all . . . raping . . . children" (as cited in Phillips, 2015, p. 66). "Does not forgive does not forget" is part of a phrase popularly quoted by the group Anonymous, while 9000 refers to a meme that was circulating amongst 4Chan and Anonymous at the time. Oprah took the post completely seriously, as did her researchers, because they did not know the language of trolls and did not bother to find out if this was a prank or not. Raping children isn't funny, but Oprah's team not recognizing a prank or doing research *is* to many people.

Communities online, if large enough, can take on a hive mentality as well—both 4Chan and Anonymous have even been referred to as part of the "Internet Hive mind," and Reddit often is said to have a controlling "hive mind." Kevin Kelley describes how in this type of large, anonymous group "more is different" in human communities in *Out of Control* (1994). In his book he notes how groups of people in the audience of a lecture can work together to hold up multi-colored sheets of paper and make patterns, comparing the people in the audience to bees in a hive. It is a simple experiment, but groups that are otherwise unknown to one another quickly figure out how to communicate by creating a pattern using their paper-based pixels. He then explores many other cases of humans coming together to work in large groups and how more people work together in differing ways from few people. The "hive mind" of the Internet has since been written about extensively; for example, Clay Shirky (2008) discusses the ability of large groups of ordinary people to economically create large scale changes and productions that were not available to them before at least briefly in many of his works. Some online groups directly use the power of swarming to create social change—Swarm Canada (swarmcanada. wordpress.com) organizes volunteers using swarm theory, for example, while Jane McGonigal's website encourages similar social change through gaming.

One of the key differences between traditional and non-traditional rhetorics online is that non-traditional rhetorics generally need groups (more than one player) to be effective. A single "player" is unlikely to defeat a mob, but more importantly, a large group that has come together to play is far more likely to be successful based upon the strategies of the current game (taunts, threats, harassment, memes, images, and so on). While other writers refer to such large groups as hives and swarms, I will call these groups of procedural (non-traditional) rhetoricians *ad-hocs*.

AD-HOCRACY

Ad-hocracy is a term that was first developed by Alvin Toffler (1984) to describe the breakdown of bureaucracy into smaller working groups that not only come together quickly to solve a problem but that break apart again just as readily when a job is done. His intention was to describe what happens in companies, but the term is equally applicable in other situations today. Bureaucracy was being recognized as soul crushing and unchanging and Toffler saw ad-hocracy as a way to change that as individuals would choose what groups to work in. While groups are seen as very important to business (and school) work today, they are not as fluid and flexible in most corporations as they are online (or as Toffler hoped they would be in business).

More recently, *ad-hocracy* became a popular term due to Cory Doctorow's 2003 novel: *Down and Out in the Magic Kingdom.* In the novel, ad-hocracies have overtaken governments and schools. Groups of people randomly come together to work on projects and break up at those projects ends. All human work is divided into these groups, and people earn not money but reputation (Whuffie) based upon their contributions and what other people think of those contributions. Essentially, *Down and Out* represents what might happen if Internet culture were writ large as our primary means of cultural construction. As the term has re-entered popular culture via the novel and is also in use in some places online, here it will be developed as a way to describe the way that groups like 4Chan and Anonymous mitigate power and form subgroups for action in chapter 2. China, in fact, created an application that gives citizens a sort of credit score based upon their interactions with social media and purchasing. If they post that the Chinese economy is doing well, for example, their score will go up, while importing anime from Japan can make their score go down. While elective in 2017, it will be required by the government in 2020. The score will affect their ability to purchase property or even receive a visa—it is essentially Whuffie (Chin & Wong, 2016).

In an ad-hocracy, it might seem that individuals and groups can rise to power fairly organically, but that does not mean that the power structure of online communities always works this way. At times the forms of online power created by ad-hocs and procedural rhetorics will look like what Jeffery Nealon (2007) refers to as Foucauldian biopower, but even if the dominant power structure online is mostly distributed, mostly about numbers, and mostly a game—that doesn't mean that people don't sometimes win through sovereign power and inflicting the harsh discipline of doxxing, *ad baculum*, and *ad hominem* on those they don't agree with. Some of the strictures of the game I will describe throughout this text can be used by individuals as well as groups, and sometimes those individuals can rule over sites and groups with near-sovereign strength.

WHAT ARE 4CHAN AND ANONYMOUS?

4Chan, one of the primary sites where trolling and ad-hocracies will be studied within this text, is an imageboard. An imageboard is a simple message board system where anyone, without registering, can post images and comments and does so, in general, without choosing a screen-name (though some people, briefly, did assign themselves names that were called "tripcodes," which have since been removed). It was based upon similar message board systems (one of which was called 2Chan) in Japan. The site opened on October 1, 2003 (Phillips, 2015) and was created by Christopher Poole—who himself remained anonymous until 2008 when he was outed by a *Wall Street Journal* article.

If you have ever, unfortunately enough, created a digital system where anybody can create a username, you can probably predict what happens on 4Chan. First, there is a lot of porn. It's hard to say whether this practice came first (trolling by filling spaces full of strange porn) or 4Chan did, but 4Chan certainly has a lot of porn on it. In fact, one of their primary guiding principles is that if it exists, there must be porn of it (Rule 34).

Figure 2. 4Chan screenshot.

Within the site itself, there are a lot of different boards (or "chans") that host a variety of different types of content. /b/ is the "random" board, and is probably the most famous for being proudly disgusting and reprehensible. On this and other boards, members continually harass one another, troll one another, make fun of one another, and generally say anything that they believe will get a reaction from other people. Because they post anonymously, people who post to 4Chan are often referred to as "anons."

Although it is a point that I will return to repeatedly, the absolute lack of moderation does mean that people say some pretty horrible things on 4Chan. Whitney Phillips (2015), a researcher who has extensively studied trolls and trolling, states that trolls on this site and others like to say *what they think is* the absolute worst thing possible—usually call someone fat, gay, some variation of "fag" or threaten rape, but it is also *the* place where most of the memes that are popular online and that have been popular online started. The members are tech savvy and quick witted, and that means that they are able to take a funny graphic somebody posts and quickly edit it, adding text or making minor changes to make it funnier (or make more variations of the same joke). This is how image macros were born (discussed in chapters 2 and 3), as well as where a lot of Internet subculture is born. You do, of course, have to wade through an awful lot of porn, hate, and nonsense to get to those things, but they are there. Furthermore, the creativity engine that 4Chan represents is not one that can simply be replicated elsewhere. Your freshman composition class is simply not going to get together on an anonymous forum and start creating memes (though with utter anonymity they might start harassing or trolling one another or you—or posting a lot of porn). However, there are elements of the structure of this system that might be used to encourage better creative practices for online spaces.

4Chan is also known to go on "raids," which is when the members of the site find another site, blog, or even Facebook user or community to harass. These raids are usually chosen by their gullibility—will the people who run the site respond negatively? If so, then the raid is probably on. 4Chan's site members will post whatever is most likely to offend or horrify the members of the raided site. Someone likes Pokémon? Post Pokémon porn! There is a "worst thing" for every possible site and every possible person.

Although anons may claim otherwise, Anonymous grew at least partly out of 4Chan's raids. According to Phillips (2015), referring to anons by the "mass noun" *Anonymous* had appeared by sometime in 2006, and by just a year later they had created their credo: "We are Anonymous, and we do not forgive" (p. 57). Anonymous was not associated with any single site as members of 4Chan are. Although originally organizing via the PartyVan Wiki, plans for raids and hacktivist activities take place via IRC channels, Facebook, and plenty of other venues as well (including some on the Deep Web). "Hacktivist" is a portmanteau used to describe their activities as being both "hacking" and "activism," these are people who at least have a minimal set of skills with network server technology or the Internet (or know how to install programs that will do things like attack servers for them) and who like to use that knowledge for social change and activism. The group is informal and fluid, with a shifting membership that is difficult to pin down because some people will join whenever they are interested in what the group is currently working on (like protesting in favor of net neutrality) and leave when they are less interested. Some of the members may choose to stay no matter the cause—some trolls are willing to troll and raid for any given reason, a certain number of Anons will become involved in any hacktivist cause available to them whether they believe in it or not. Initially these raids were very similar to those conducted by 4Chan—one was against a woman that was both a grade school teacher and an online dominatrix and another was at the social networking (for young people) site Habbo Hotel. These targets were often single individuals or groups that were easy to rile up and get "lulz" from ("lulz" are essentially laughter derived from *schadenfreude*). They used the singular group noun Anonymous to describe themselves—by using the same name they could gain a great deal of power for that name.

Early actions by Anonymous against individuals were followed by more positive raids on groups. When Anonymous turned their group energy to attacking organizations (mostly) instead of individuals (again, mostly), it represented a bigger shift in their focus. They became more liberal and began to work on defending individuals against media, religious, political, and social organizations that they viewed as particularly corrupt. Phillips (2015) sees this shift as beginning when Fox News reported on Anonymous in 2007 calling them "Hackers on steroids" (p. 58). The report was the first time that Anonymous was referred to in popular press as regarding the net as a "real life video game"—which is perhaps one of the only parts of the report that was accurate as the rest was filled with hyperbole and fear-mongering. In the report, Phil Shuman called Anonymous the "Internet hate machine," a moniker that stuck, and went on to call them "domestic terrorists" (qtd. in Phillips, 2015, p. 58). The report was posted to YouTube and began a troll raid against Fox News. Both 4Chan and Anonymous got a lot of attention from the report, and it was not all negative. People who wanted to join in on the "lulz" naturally visited 4Chan, sometimes for the first time, as a direct result of the story. If Fox News wanted to stop Anonymous, it would have been hard for them to create a worse story to do so.

Aside from which, Fox News's reporting on Anonymous was already woefully behind target. At that time Anonymous's raids were against white supremacists (Hal Turner, a white supremacist talk radio host, had his website targeted) and Internet predators (Chris Forcand). They moved on to form a giant raid including real life protests of the Church of Scientology, called Project Chanology, and would later be involved in WikiLeaks.

Anonymous has become more political. In 2014, they posted warnings to the Ferguson, Missouri police that shamed them for the death of Michael Brown and threatened them if any protestors were harmed. They were involved in "doxxing" the police as well—they posted to the Web the personal details such as address information of police officers in the St. Louis area who were involved in the case and also outed members of the local police force who were members of (or had family in) white supremacist organizations. In 2015, they took a renewed stand against pedophiles online, and also attacked white supremacist website Stormfront.

For an organization that grew out of a site that made a lot of memes but also hosts a lot of porn, racism, and misogyny, Anonymous has become an online power that is *mostly* against racism and sometimes against misogyny. 4Chan remains 4Chan—a site for trolling and memes, but without it trolling rhetoric would not have developed, many of the best memes would not have been created, and Anonymous would have never gotten its start.

At the same time, a conservative flavor of troll has taken to what is currently referred to as the "Alt-Right." While Anonymous fights white supremacy, these trolls are drawn to it. Using trolling language as well as memes, sites like *The Daily Stormer* represent the interests of white supremacy as well as men's rights organizations and present themselves as conservative news outlets. While Phillips (2015) and others have successfully argued that trolls don't take their online selves seriously, it would be dangerous to assume the same of all organizations that have either co-opted trolling rhetoric or attracted Alt-Right trolls.

The Rules of the Internet and "Serious Business"

Serious Business. Whether or not Anonymous and 4Chan can be "good," or even effective, in Biting Beaver's case they were both effective and a negative influence during their attacks and raids while during the rape cases they were a positive and effective force. There are two primary governing ideas that trolls and large ad-hocs mostly seem to abide and form by, and both are determining factors in who they decide to target, who to support, and how the rest of their procedural rhetorics are formulated. These two factors are a phrase and a list: "The Internet is Serious Business" and the Rules of the Internet (4Chan, /b/, 2011).

The first phrase is used commonly online (and reached peak popularity between 2005–2011), but it is important to understand that it is meant ironically or sarcastically. When a post or website is responded to with any variation of the Internet being "Serious Business," what is truly being implied is that the individual is either using the Internet in a non-playful, far too serious way, or they are taking the opinions of others online as being desperately important (Encyclopedia Dramatica, 2010). If you are too visibly hurt by something that is said about you online, you become a more attractive target to trolls for taking their harassment "seriously." When Fox News reads something from a troll on the air, this is the best thing that could ever happen to that troll—someone took the trolling they posted as factual. This phrase (or some variation of it, such as "serious business" or "serous bizness" or some other abbreviation or misspelling) can be attached to a complex argument on an Internet forum, a website that is trying to use the Internet to persuade or teach people about something complex and highly political, and in some cases it is said with a graphic similar to a meme that has the words on it in some way (Encyclopedia Dramatica, "The Internet is Serious Business," 2010). The phrase started on 4Chan but has since spread far beyond the site's borders.

It is important to note that what is really being argued is that the Internet should never be taken too seriously by participants. Does it really matter if someone is "wrong" online? While the Internet is part of "real life," should it really be as important or judged as equivalent to it? Anonymous and 4Chan (amongst other groups and people) would argue that this medium was never meant for serious purposes to begin with, and although we have tried to use it for such, many of those uses have failed rhetorically. Social media, Facebook, Twitter, cat pictures—these are the "native" genres to digital systems that have grown out of Internet practices, and they can also be very rhetorically persuasive (and, ironically enough, they can be so about "serious topics").

What is *really* implied by "the Internet is serious business" is one of two things: either (A) you reacted too strongly to an attack by another individual online or (B) you are posting in essay-ist logic or classical/ traditional rhetoric in spaces that essays and classical rhetoric just don't fit easily. Phillips (2015) writes:

> Trolls believe that nothing should be taken seriously, and therefore regard public displays of sentimentality, political conviction, and/ or ideological rigidity as a call to trolling arms. In this way, lulz functions as a pushback against any and all forms of attachment, a highly ironic stance given how attached trolls are to the pursuit of lulz. (2015, p. 25)

Phillips traces trolls' attachment to trolling to lulz specifically, instead of simply to the outcome. Trolls seem to believe that if they keep at something long enough lulz must be generated eventually when their target becomes worn down, and they are generally right.

Phillips (2015) traces trolls' use of "serious business" also to their mask of emotional dissociation. The troll is logical to a fault, and the only emotion that should enter into a bout of trolling is that laughter that occurs when a target gets emotional or takes the trolling seriously. She ties this concept to Gregory Bateson's "play frame," which is what occurs when friends or people who are otherwise acquaintances use bodily movement, tone of voice, and language to indicate that something said should be taken in jest rather than seriously (Bateson, 1972). I always imagined this as being similar to a dog's play bow—after the butt is up and front legs are down the growling that comes after is not actually a fight. Phillips calls the persona that people take on when trolling their "trolling mask" (not unlike a Guy Fawkes mask that many wear in physical protests), and suggests that the problem with trolling behavior is not that it is play, but that it is play that the other person does not recognize as play:

> Trolling establishes a similar frame, but unlike Bateson's account, which implies good faith and reciprocal engagement, the mask worn by trolls precludes reciprocity; only the troll can wear the mask. The recipient of the trolls' playful behavior, on the other hand, is expected to take things seriously, the more seriously the better. If the target does not, then the troll has failed. (Phillips, 2015, p. 33)

In other words—trolls are playing, but only the trolls know it.

The Rules of the Internet. The Rules of the Internet are harder to trace than the "Internet is Serious Business" because the dates cited for the list's creation on sites like Urban Dictionary and Encyclopedia Dramatica do not match my own dates of phrases from the rules being used against BB and even earlier targets. Additionally, many different versions of the list exist—although they all hold several of the rules in common. The list started as rules for anonymous posters raiding on other sites and was discussed on 4Chan. Encyclopedia Dramatica (2013) traces the list back to 2007, but my own research shows that some of these phrases were in use as early as 2005–2006. Additionally, Encyclopedia Dramatica entries from before 2011 were lost and rebuilt, which means that many articles might have been more accurate before that date. The list starts in a *Fight Club*-esque (Palahniuk, 1996) fashion—"1. Do not talk about /b/. 2. Do NOT talk about /b/"—then moves into a definition of what Anonymous is—"3. We are Anonymous. 4. Anonymous is legion. 5. Anonymous never forgives. 6. Anonymous can be a senseless, horrible, uncaring monster. 7.

Anonymous is still able to deliver" (Encyclopedia Dramatica, 2009). Rules 3–7 are often repeated when raids are ongoing and now appear in many of the videos that Anonymous has made to talk about their various activities and warn targets of impending raids.

Although the Rules were created for and by 4Chan and Anonymous, the list or parts of it are often referenced in other widespread message-board communities and paired with images. For example, Rule 34—"There is porn of it, no exceptions"—is extremely popular. Because the Rules are one of the most easily accessible entrances to being an Anon, people who are new to the site and want to get involved have a tendency to either over-quote the rules or take them too seriously, attempting to enforce them upon Anonymous and 4Chan as well as other sites. In general, this practice is frowned upon, so although the Rules are really a list of the most common memes that 4Chan and Anonymous have been known for, they may not be internally enforced because doing so is often done by new people (aka newbs).

There are only forty-seven rules according to Encyclopedia Dramatica. The extended list contains more references to pop culture including video games (Rule 66: "The cake is a lie" references *Portal*, for example [Grimies, 2010]) and television (Rule 90, "It's never lupus," references *House* (Grimies, 2010)).

The most important rules are simple: nothing is to be taken seriously, and there is always porn of it.

Despite their intrinsic edit-ability and some Anons sometimes claiming they don't matter (because *nothing* matters), the Rules are perhaps one of the best guides to what has been popular online for the past eight years as well as how to behave to not get oneself targeted by either 4Chan or Anonymous. They should not be confused with the procedures used in trolling directly—those will be discussed in a later chapter.

Trolling. Online trolls, flame wars, and hackers have been discussed at some length in past publications as well. However, many such writings are not in tune with current Internet practices (largely due to the quick-changing nature of technology and online culture). Similarly, many books that look explicitly at flames, trolls, and hackers are now also out of date. The collection *Flame Wars* (1994) is a good example. This book provides a good history of how flames have been used over time and can be used as a comparative piece to communities today, but there is very little similarity between the rape that Julian Dibbell

(1998) writes about in early online communities and the ease with which "raep" is used by current message-board users. Even this study will someday be historical—and I would urge others to continue to study these flashpoints as potentially important points of study for rhetoricians as they allow us to track both effective and ineffective online rhetoric.

More recent (and accurate) studies of trolls are not all academic studies. While I venture that they are more accurate (and more true to my own experiences and studies), many are unprofessionally published or focused on areas not of interest to this study. For example, following the trend of the earlier text *Virtual Justice* (Lakatowa, 2010), many of these texts are focused on protecting businesses or professionals from trolls (Gonciarz, 2012). They see the primary issue of trolling (a term given two provenances: first that it refers to nasty fairy tale creatures that live under bridges and second that it refers to trolling for fish—using a boat and other equipment to encourage fish to bite) as it being destructive to the victim's reputation (whether that be a company or individual). While harm to reputation is certainly important and worth discussing with students, the tips given by these texts for protecting reputation do not protect against emotional harm or help an individual win an argument against trolls or even learn to use trolling methods for social good instead of ill. Most of these sources casually nod towards the ability of ad-hocracy techniques being potentially useful for social good, but they focus on the horrors created in much more detail. After all—if you want to sell a book to a corporation and get them to hire you as a consultant, scaring them is a must. They also completely fail to help the individual reader find a comfortable place online from which to play, write, and argue—again because some of the authors are available for hire or because the authors themselves have yet to find a technique that would be effective.

In *U Mad? The Internet's Guide to Idiots*, Christopher Gonciarz (2012) suggests that things go wrong online all the time. Most users will, at some point or another, misuse their power online probably without realizing it. Studying how fallacious arguments may have become procedural could help users realize when they are using this style of rhetoric since it is so enmeshed in the community itself. Gonciarz (2012) also believes that everyone who writes and publishes online needs to be more responsible for showing users appropriate role models in online writing and multimedia production. Gonciarz seems to want to stop trolling through careful community standards, which given why and how trolls function is probably unlikely to be entirely successful.

Similarly, Andrea Weckerle's text, *Civility in the Digital Age* (2013), defines many different types of trolls and attacks, and suggests that anonymity online is important for many social movements, and discusses "online lynch mobs"—essentially what I will be referring to as ad-hocracies or ad-hocs throughout this text. While Weckerle primarily looks at "lynch-mobs" as performing unnecessary attacks against innocent individuals, I will also look at groups forming that have positive goals. Some people have taken lessons learned from trolls and trolling and already turned them towards positive means. This does not mean, however, that we can ignore how utterly destroyed the lives are of the individuals targeted. Once a message is sent—and others latch onto it—it seemingly takes on a life of its own. You cannot stop related ad-hocs from "helping" in ways you did not already intend. The group isn't really controllable, so considering consequences early should be part of any planning process that involves them.

Civility in a Digital Age (2013) is also useful because Weckerle discusses ways of dealing with trolls and hate online other than simply ignoring them. Common advice online includes "do not feed the trolls." In other words, if you or your site come under attack, trolls should be ignored and they will go away. While this is true in some instances, it is certainly not always effective. The Church of Scientology, for example, attempted to ignore Anonymous when they began to attack the website and protest at physical locations. However, trolls aren't stupid—if they are loud enough you will have to respond. *How* to respond, then, is key. Weckerle recommends disempowering trolls through posting their identification when it can be determined (usually called "doxxing" for the posting of documents) or simply banning them from sites. However, this is not always enough. Other writers (Sweeney, 2013) note that banning does not always work because users can easily create more log-ins to most websites, and even sites that are supposed to prevent users from doing so—like Facebook—rarely completely prevent it. Furthermore, doxxing can be deeply destructive to an individual's future ability to find work as well as their personal safety. It's easy to imagine that people "deserve it" if they have been trolls themselves, but some journalists that have hunted down trolls for interviews have found that that is simply not true. One troll reportedly sent most of his comments to his target (an overweight woman with a blog about weight) when he, himself, was struggling with depression and his own weight. It should not surprise us that hate is often fueled by insecurity, but it is easy to forget that the troll might not entirely agree with what they are posting, or might—in time—come to regret what they have said even without being doxxed.

Oisín Sweeney (2013) has written a text specifically addressing one type of trolling that occurs online that has grown directly out of 4Chan. At times his book, *Hackers on Steroids*, like many non-academic studies of trolling and flame wars, is a completely honest look at just how awful online conversations can be. However, Sweeney seems to hold a far too personal grudge against the trolls that he profiles and even submits them to some of their own tactics within the text itself, making it less a study of troll behavior or exposé and more a rant about trolls' existence. While I recognize these tactics as being effective, I would not recommend vigilante justice as a preferably imitated form of procedural rhetoric as Sweeney would.

The most definitive study of trolling is Whitney Phillips' *This is Why We Can't Have Nice Things: Mapping the Relationship between Online Trolling and Mainstream Culture* (2015). Phillips studied trolls for several years and interviewed many as well. Instead of simply witnessing and judging trollish behavior, Phillips infiltrated trolling planning groups on Facebook, began to understand the humor of trolling herself, interviewed trolls, and gave a balanced analysis of their place in the media landscape. However, she at times notes that quoting trolls and describing their exploits is a fine line to walk. When writing about this phenomenon, a certain amount of offensive content is necessary to describe what has been written, posted, and talked about. At the same time, she describes herself as "reluctant to uncritically replicate trolls' racist, sexist, homophobic, and ablest output" (2015, p. 2). At best, I think it is impossible to adequately describe trolling and the nature of 4Chan and Anonymous without quoting some of the memes, slang, and other pieces of their lexicon within one's analysis. Were one to use this, or her, study as a historical piece in the future, I would not want them to see a cleaned-up version of any of these events. It should be clear that the rhetorics discussed within these pages are devious, dirty, sarcastic, infantile, and at times just gross—but that is a part of their culture that is just as important as pictures of cats are.

Phillips' primary thesis is that trolls provide "an implicit, and sometimes outright explicit, critique of existing media and cultural systems" (2015, p. 7). Trolling embodies "American" values such as freedom of speech, and also tends to "replicate gendered notions of dominance and success" (2015, p. 8). However, trolls do this through an adversarial method that Phillips likens to the Trickster. The troll is mischievous and wants to lead the person being trolled into their own ruin (Coleman, 2012). Phillips argues that trolling behaviors are simply an extreme form of normal behaviors. Trolls like to point out mistakes made by the media, but they also like to get their own material into the media (the Oprah story is legendary). Phillips argues that

> trolls are born of and embedded within dominant institutions and tropes, which are every bit as damaging as the trolls' most disruptive behaviors. Ultimately, then, this is why we can't have nice things, and is the point to which the title gestures: the fact that online trolling is par for the mainstream cultural course. (2015, p. 11)

Our media, she posits, is just as dangerous as trolls. Our current news media tends toward shrill excess. When a hacker guessed the password for Sarah Palin's yahoo e-mail address, O'Reilly called 4Chan (the site claiming credit) "one of those despicable, slimy, scummy websites," which only urged the trolls to try harder to get mentioned by the media.

But their coverage of trolling is not the only problem that Phillips identifies. The media needs a spectacle in order to survive, and 4Chan and Anonymous take advantage of that fact by providing that spectacle. One need only to think of the media circuses surrounding the 2016 election to understand the ways in which our media is driven by ad revenue and click-throughs, especially when fake news can circulate and generate both. Trolls and media outlets push for success—they want to win the game (Phillips, 2015). When journalists are exploitative, this is just seen as normal. However, when trolls are exploitative, they are "condemned as aberrational" (2015, p. 68). She believes that by giving journalists a free pass the most problematic behaviors of trolling will continue as they serve to highlight that exploitation.

She refers to the type of trolls that exist on 4Chan and Reddit as "subcultural trolls" (Phillips, 2015). Trolling existed before the types of trolls that she studies. The trolls studied here come from one of two ad-hocs (with occasional crossover to Reddit)—4Chan and Anonymous. They are creators of memes and language that is used widely elsewhere on the web, and their anonymous, unmoderated discussion is an incubator for a lot of the cultural capital that the web possesses. She describes trolls' purpose as being to "disrupt and upset as many people as possible, using whatever linguistic or behavioral tools are available" (Phillips, 2015, p. 2). This echoes, to a certain extent, Aristotle's definition of rhetoric: "the faculty of observing in any given case the available means of persuasion" (*Rhetoric*, 1.2). The means available to trolls are simply different, and they have chosen to make different use of them than the average rhetorician. This does not make them any less rhetorical.

Procedural Rhetoric. As I mentioned earlier, I believe that gaming rhetoric—that is, *procedural rhetoric*—has a place in describing the rhetorical moves made by many of those who argue online via trolling and ad-hocs. The most famous text about gaming rhetoric is easily Ian Bogost's *Persuasive Games* (2007) wherein procedural rhetoric is defined and demonstrated, though limited to gaming. Procedural rhetoric is "the art of persuasion through rule-based representations and interactions rather than the spoken word, writing, images, or moving pictures" (Bogost, 2007, p. ix). It is any rhetoric that makes use of the things that make computer mediated communication and persuasion unique: "Computers run processes, they execute calculations and rule-based symbolic manipulations" (Bogost, 2007, p. ix). Bogost goes on to claim, however, that video games have a unique kind of procedural power that Word, say, might not (on the other hand, Selfe and Selfe (1994) argue that the GUI of any software is itself rhetorical—but this rhetorical-activity comes from the visual graphic user interface itself, not specifically from just procedures). Some trolls use *processes* in their persuasion—they follow a formula and in so doing they can be successful. The Oprah troll was not particularly witty nor did he make a new claim. Instead, the troll reposted (the term is "copypasta") from a few different memes onto a message board and got that message read on live television by Oprah Winfrey. That is proceduralism at work—if you meme it, they will come.

Bogost notes that other pieces of software are used to create rhetoric, while computer-based video games seem to embody it. They rely upon the computer to bear meaning and persuade, they do not exist outside of the machine:

> Video games are computational artifacts that have cultural meaning *as* computational artifacts. Moreover, they are a popular form of computation artifact, perhaps the most prevalent for of expressive computation. Video games are thus a particularly relevant medium for computational persuasion and expression. (2007, p. ix)

However, Bogost limits many of his examples to political and educational games that many readers would never play unless they had read his text. Since it is not immediately apparent that these examples can be applied beyond these very specifically rhetorical games (and even beyond games themselves), the application of this theory outside of games is unclear. Bogost's work is instrumental in understanding how rhetoric by procedure is possible, however.

Other games studies scholars have studied and defined rhetorical moves and situations within other parts of games. McAllister's *Game Work* (2004) looks at rhetoric within games and as games are being created. For example, rhetoric surrounds the development of games, is present in their text, is used by their creators when talking about the game, and exists in reviews of games. McCallister does note that the ubiquity of gaming terms in our society, as does Wark (2007). Wark's philosophical piece, *Gamer Theory*, suggests that such language has built a situation wherein we are always in a game—much as Plato's Cave allegorized the idea that we are always being told a story and being persuaded. If everything is already part of gamespace (just as we are always already cyborgs), then we can certainly view Internet conversations through a lens of gaming.

This is with good reason. Computers have a distinct relationship with games—it is almost as if their logic was built for them. Indeed, computers in general share what Jesper Juul calls a "basic affinity" with games:

> Like the printing press and cinema have historically promoted and enabled new kinds of storytelling, computers work as enablers of games, letting us play old games in new ways, and allowing for new types of games that would previously not have been possible. (2005, p. 5)

Whether or not this basic affinity changed the way we argue with one another when introduced to networked argumentation might not ever be clear—for example, we could also, and often do, blame anonymity—but these new kinds of storytelling and play have certainly enabled new kinds of conversations and arguments. Other texts, such as Flanagan's *Critical Play* (2009), take the things we have learned about Serious Games and use them to recommend game design elements that will help people learn to be critical thinkers, persuade them on political topics, and learn about the world around them. I, myself, am not taking the lessons learned from studying the communities I do back into game design. Instead, I take the lessons I learn from studying gaming rhetoric in non-gaming environments into teaching writing and understanding rhetoric for those non-gaming digital environments. The assignments that I create and will report on in chapter 5 use elements of Serious Games and game design, but are not ultimately games themselves (well, mostly anyway).

More than a decade has passed since our foundational studies created the academic Internet as we understand it, and things have changed—our students are no longer spending their free time creating characters for MUDs, instead they probably spend more time in MMORGPS like *World of Warcraft*; they chat with their friends via instant messaging systems built into Facebook and via their phones rather than using AOL Instant Messenger or even large anonymous chatrooms; they blog or post on Tumblr more often than they hand-code personal webpages in HTML; and they are probably well-versed (at least some of them) in the Rules of the Internet even if they are not consciously aware of being schooled in them at any point. These new experiences are the socially embedded practices that students bring with them whenever we ask them to use Internet technology in the classroom.

These are just some reasons that some of them think Internet technology is not for them. They live connected to their phones but don't see that as part of the Internet. They may very well have been burned by past experiences as well. These students deserve to learn not just survival skills for online communities (because who wants to simply survive?), but new methods and new rhetorics for thriving online and building online communities for themselves.

CHAPTERS DESCRIPTION

In chapter 2, I define and explore ad-hocracy in depth. I then examine why large (massive) message board systems are different than the small communities that we build in classrooms (and why those small communities are not good preparation for the rhetoric students might face in those communities). Exploring a concept first introduced by Toffler—the ad-hocracy—and later described by Kevin Kelley—"more is different"—lately made popular by books like *Wikinomics* (2006), *Here Comes Everybody* (2008), and *Cognitive Surplus* (2010), I argue that massive audiences like those present in MMORPGs and large message board systems like 4Chan, Reddit, and the older Metafilter feature gamic elements in their rhetoric. I focus upon disagreement, the use of puns, imagery, and large group action in regards to racist and sexist statements in both games *and* communities with many thousands of users. These elements of gaming allow users to take action as a community by quickly forming ad-hocracies and raising money, attacking "enemies" online, and becoming politically active rather than simply learning how to defeat bosses and work together as a team.

In chapter 3, I define the Internet as a game (through a lens of gaming) so that procedural rhetoric might be applied to it. Following that definition, I provide analysis of why procedural rhetoric pairs so well with the sorts of online groups that have formed around it.

In chapter 4, I discuss the ways that the Game of the Internet is built through specific procedural rhetorical tropes. These tropes are those that are action-orientated, and many of them have real world consequences. For example, I look at how people are taught to "dox" one another and perform DDoS (distributed denial of service) attacks. In chapter 5, then, I look at more lexical tropes that procedural rhetoric is built upon. Specifically, I examine how trolls use Socrates, Arthur Schopenhauer, and the media itself to build procedural rhetoric.

In chapter 6, I tie the previous information into composition pedagogy. How can the lessons learned by looking at Internet communities and conversations as games be brought into the composition classroom? Should they? In this chapter I present several assignments that expand upon gaming in composition pedagogy to not only present a rhetoric of play, but to take advantage of procedural rhetoric and teach students how to use procedural rhetoric in digital writing. These assignments were used in sections of Technical Writing and Applied Digital Writing at Frostburg State University, as well as past classes at Wayne State University and Baker College, with the results reported in the chapter. I will discuss possibilities for creating online communities for face-to-face, hybrid, online, and even MOOC courses that could engage students through procedural rhetorics—which most of our current activities via message boards, wikis, and blogs for students simply do not.

2 Ad-hocracies

To begin to discuss how treating the Internet as a game not only changes our communication on it but also our rhetoric, I would like to first discuss groups like Anonymous that *game* the Internet the most and how these groups create and redefine Internet culture and use gaming rhetorics. Anonymous is just the most known (and best organized) of such ad-hocracies.

Large websites with millions of participants, mostly pseudo-anonymous or entirely anonymous, have their own cultures, to be sure, but the ones I would like to study and theorize about are those that effect the rest of the Web. In this case, some of them also create media that is not only viewable but popularized far and wide—primarily memes. These sites tend to be the places that viral media is created, and they also happen to be mostly anonymous.

Even if you have never spent any time on 4Chan or Reddit, you have probably read or viewed content first created or disseminated by people on one of these sites. This has only gotten more prevalent as news organizations and meme aggregators (even Buzzfeed) steal material, memes, and polls from Reddit and 4Chan and popularize them. As noted in chapter 1, many of the people who spend lots of time on 4Chan or used to spend time on Anonymous's PartyVan Wiki also "troll" people elsewhere on the Web, but they also have created many of the memes that are popular. A meme is an idea, picture, idea, behavior, style—a thing—that spreads from person to person within a culture; it is a simple unit of cultural exchange (Dawkins, 1976). Today, we mostly use this term to describe images and text juxtapositions that are humorous and repeatable. Memes have gained popularity online—members of the general public who have never read Richard Dawkins' work are familiar with the term—but they existed before the Internet. However, the Internet allows them to become very popular very quickly and to have lasting affects across many different subcultures. For example, cat macros—cute pictures of cats paired with white, blocky, often misspelled text—were first popularized on 4Chan on "Caturdays." Caturdays were a weekly event wherein people visiting the site would post pictures of cats on Saturdays. Because they were funny, clever, and easy to create they gained widespread popularity online, and today many different similar forms of "image macro" memes can be found on nearly every message or discussion board that allows image posting or linking. Other people have readapted the cat meme to include pictures of critical theorists, dogs, babies, and almost any other type of photo that someone can put the same style of text over.

The same mechanism by which 4Chan can create a funny, new, popular meme also allows them to be very effective trolls and for Anonymous to take social action against others online and even in the "real world." They do so by creating "ad-hocracies," or "ad-hocs."

As noted in chapter 1, *ad-hocracy* is a term that was first developed by Alvin Toffler (1971) to describe the breakdown of bureaucracies into smaller working groups that come together quickly to solve a problem and then break apart just as quickly. He saw ad-hocracy as the ultimate way that people would change the soul-crushing, unchanging-ness that bureaucracy created. The term has become popular again in the 2000's because of inclusion in Corey Doctorow's novel *Down and Out in the Magic Kingdom* (2003), wherein all human work is centered around these sorts of groups that form and disperse based upon need. One way to describe the way people get work done online is to suggest that they work in such ad-hocs. The most successful online groups persuade *as a group*, not as an individual. The nameless, faceless horde of Anonymous speaks with one single voice—and is all the more powerful for it. They are not Anonymous—made up of five thousand different people—they are *Anonymous*, and they function as one.

Doctorow's (2003) novel expands upon Toffler's definition in many ways, cleverly adding in concepts from the Internet. Doctorow's main character, Julius, lives in a future America that has been taken over by the so-called "Bitchun Society." Ad-Hocracy grew, in the novel, from a group of people that wanted to break free from the crushing bureaucracy that had overtaken places like Walt Disney World and other large corporations. The ad-hocs honestly believed that they could run institutions like airlines, theme parks, and universities better than the current administration. Likewise, Anonymous believes that in some cases vigilante justice better protects and helps people than governmental intervention—where the government fails, an ad-hoc might succeed. At least in the novel, they weren't far from the truth—the ad-hocs were able to take over society. This is partially because the Bitchun Society has done away with money, and now focuses their efforts upon earning "Whuffie"—electronic brownie points earned by being popular. Ideas worth a lot of Whuffie are those that people respect the most. Having the best ideas in any ad-hoc, therefore, makes you the best and most respected person in that ad-hoc. You also become the one with the most cash. Doctorow refers to this as a "meritocracy," and it is related to the ratings systems that many message boards currently employ. Every time you click the upvote button on Reddit or Digg, link to someone's post, or "Like" something on Facebook, you are contributing to just such a meritocracy. Doctorow's ideas were far more extraordinary in 2003 when the book was first released—Facebook had just been released in 2004, the Like button hadn't been created yet, and real meritocracies online were years away. However, it has proven nearly clairvoyant in some respects, even if meritocracy has not flowed into the "real world" as much as it has online. A whuffie app that determines your social capital based upon social media sites like Twitter has been created, but sadly did not have much buy in.

Despite that, there are real world uses of ad-hocs and even gaming theory in schools and corporations today. For example, *gamification* has been a contested concept in games studies but has become popular in some businesses and schools (Bogost, 2011). Just about anything can be made into a game by making certain outcomes (write a paper, get a new client, update the website) worth points and prizes. Making work a game is meant to increase performance and encourage workers to complete work faster. In reality, it may encourage them to get tasks done faster but not better—and just like video games, some people attempt to cheat as well. Even in Internet communities that function with upvotes, certain types of posts (funny, gross, etc.) are likely to "win" and get the most votes instead of posts with a lot of "content." Because of this, gamification is ultimately seen as something useful but ultimately not a reliable way to run a society or even to use in games. Instead, games theorists like Bogost (2011; 2015) suggest that we try to move past gamification to find other ways to bring games into systems, and might even see gamification as dangerous (Bogost's argument in 2011 contained the idea that gamification—giving prizes for performance—was partly behind the real estate market collapse of 2008). A quickly brought together ad-hoc, such as that formed when you find other people to play difficult raids, bosses, or dungeons with in games like *World of Warcraft*, might be one way to do so.

Ad-Hocs brought together by a singular goal can be very effective—they have a lot of energy, but can be villainous in nature as easily as they can be chivalrous. Even in Doctorow's novel, ad-hocs can run a theme park, design new rides, and so on, but they don't always preserve the past very well. In the book, this is represented by the ad-hocs wishing to tear down old attractions and replace them with new ones. If all members of a group are only worried about getting some work done now they might not be as concerned as they need to be about preservation instead of replacement. Preservation of past ideals and projects is also not very terribly important to the online ad-hocs that I have researched—their focus is very much on the present, and past "raids" are rarely returned to. In some cases this is good, but it also means that old raids don't get followed up on when new developments happen. In the case of 4Chan, they actively do not archive their work or their site—once the writing is gone off the bottom of the screen it is gone forever. Some websites have sprung up for the exclusive purpose of archiving 4Chan, but a user must request that a certain board over a certain time period be archived—they don't simply save everything in the same way that the Internet Archive itself does.

The second description of a hostile ad-hoc takeover that Doctorow writes is set, interestingly enough, in a university (2003). A group of sociology graduate students forcefully takes over the department. He notes that when people fight back it rarely goes well for them. Doctorow writes that a professor was on stage lecturing at the time the takeover occurred. The graduate students formed a human wall in front of the professor, took his microphone, and began to lecture themselves:

> Come on, heads up! This is *not* a drill. This University of Toronto Department of Sociology is under new management . . . Before I start though, I have a prepared statement for you . . . Here goes: We reject the stodgy, tyrannical rule of the profs at this Department. We demand bully pulpits from which to preach the Bitchun gospel. Effective immediately, the University of Toronto Ad-Hoc Sociology Department is *in charge*. We promise a high-relevance curriculum with an emphasis on reputation economies, post-scarcity social dynamics, and the social theory of infinite life-extension. No more Durkheim, kids, just deadheading! This will be *fun*. (Doctorow, 2003, p.174)

Such hostile takeovers are pretty common online, where hackers can break into someone's website and post their own content. As described earlier, hundreds and thousands of trolls sometimes also descend onto a single website to get the owner or community members to leave, shut it down, or stop posting. To demonstrate this concept, Doctorow (2003) simply took this sort of action into the real world. However, just as happens online, usually it is the sites themselves that are harmed in the process of a takeover—especially if the original owners fight back and fail. In the confusion, not a lot of learning takes place.

AD-HOCS IN THE REAL WORLD

These days anons are not only involved online. Although they organize online (more often via IRC chatrooms, Twitter, and other social networks than the afore-mentioned "PartyVan Wiki"), they also plan staged protests in public wearing Guy Fawkes' masks, which are named after the lead character in the film *V for Vendetta*.

They are not just "hackers" who hack into systems for fun, money, or because they can, they are also "hacktivists" who have fun and take great pride in enacting social change. 4Chan seems to have largely taken over harassing "social justice warriors" in the ways that Anonymous earlier did, while splinter groups from 4Chan have firmly joined the Alt-Right. Whether or not 4Chan can develop in the same ways that Anonymous has remains unseen—perhaps the format is just too chaotic for a different perspective to work.

Phillips (2015) writes about this shift in Anonymous as well. Trolling can be used to influence the media and draw attention to corruption in governments worldwide. Phillips traces this shift to the entry of the trolling lexicon and its memes into the mainstream—you can buy meme t-shirts at popular chain stores like Spencer's and Hot Topic, for example, and schools are opening up websites where students are invited to make memes about the institutions. As larger groups recognize the power of meme creation, it seems to make sense that they would harness that power for themselves (after all—that is one of the things I suggest might need to happen to creativity in classrooms in chapter 6).

Anonymous and Rape Culture. Imagine that you are a young girl living in a small town in America. You decided to go to a party being held by the popular kids in your (or an adjacent) high school. This is a *big deal*—your chance at "making it" in a town where football is still worshipped, Main Street still has a holdout General Store not yet turned into a Dollar General, and where many people grow up and go to college, but never really leave. Nothing seems more important than this invitation to hang out with cute boys, maybe get to drink, and be part of the crowd that controls what seems like "everything" in your fairly small world.

In a story that is all too familiar, you wake up the next morning in pain, disorientated, with few memories of the night before. If you are lucky, you made it home, even if your parents had to help you inside. Classmates fill you in about how messed up you were, make fun of you for your behavior, and ultimately blame you for what happened. "What happened," in the cases discussed here, is rape. Due to the ubiquity of cell phone cameras and social networking, you can find images of yourself and trace the night boys took advantage of you drunk. If you or your family decides to go to the police then these images and videos should be supportive of your case, no matter how painful and awful they are to look at.

It's a small town though, and not only does the case go stale very quickly, but as soon as you do press charges abuse begins again. Everyone is friends with everyone else, and everyone seems to think you are the person "making trouble," completely ignoring that you are the one trouble happened to. You want the name-calling and threats to go away. Maybe the case is dropped entirely. You might even start doubting yourself.

The *last* people you would expect to support you and help bring the other students that did this to you to justice is Anonymous—the same people who just a few years ago harassed several feminists completely off of the Internet. Anonymous was seemingly just telling women to get back in the kitchen, and yet here they are talking about rape culture?

As unbelievable as it seems, a group that got its start by organizing to harass people online, whose earliest targets counted among them an IT specialist who was overcharging people for basic services and so-called "Feminazis," now has new targets—primarily governmental cover-ups, bullies, conservative media like Fox News, and corporate corruption. This development has not been sudden—it demonstrates the ability of ad-hocs to shift focus. However, for the game the ad-hoc is playing to continue, there must always be an enemy.

Anonymous helped attract media attention to several recent rape cases that would have otherwise gone on being overlooked (and they were far more successful in doing so than most Title IX investigations).

For example, a girl from a town near Steubenville, Ohio was dragged drunk to several parties held by popular students of Steubenville High shortly before the fall term (and football season) began (Oppel, 2013). The boys eventually charged in the case were football players. People at the parties took and posted pictures of the girl to various social media sites, texted each other, and even posted to Twitter about the events. Because of the large amount of video and photographic evidence, the case should have been easy to prosecute. In many photos the girl was clearly passed out and being carried. Students witnessed others raping the girl and joking about doing so. She was referred to as "looking dead" (Davidson, 2013).

The girl's family and police were not able to gather as many of the pictures and videos as existed (when other students realized there might be a case they not only closed ranks to protect their star athletes, they also naturally deleted a lot of the evidence and did not want to be caught with it). Anonymous's contribution was to find and post publicly those images and videos, saying that doing so would make it all but impossible for police and prosecutors to ignore the case. Because Anonymous has in its ranks at least some fairly accomplished hackers, retrieving deleted images that might be part of someone's iPhone Photo Stream is just as easy when trying to prosecute a rapist as when they might be looking for celebrity nude photos to distribute.

Although it is impossible to define exactly who is part of an ad-hoc (especially one in which all members value anonymity because some of their actions defy legality), almost all "anons" who have been interviewed online or on broadcast media are young males who enjoy computers—many of whom could be considered to be "geeks." As a group, they pick targets by cases that have upset the greatest number of them. No single member should use the group as their "own personal army" according to the Rules of the Internet, so there is not a leader that can point them in a direction him or herself. In this case, it was not so much that a girl was raped that angered them, but instead that she was made fun of and bullied for it afterwards. Students and other people in the small town accused her of trying to ruin the team's season, of being promiscuous, and of making it all up because she regretted what happened in the morning—all fairly predictable ways of silencing rape victims. As a group, even though Anonymous can sometimes be online bullies themselves, they completely hate bullying in general. As of Fall 2015, they currently seem to want to defend the so-called "little guy" from the government, corporations, and even small town politics. Anonymous is happy to target a city, government, or organization that uses power unwisely or to punish less powerful people, but posting the identities of people who committed crimes as minors and calling for vigilante justice might not be the safest way to do so for all parties involved.

In the Steubenville case, Anonymous not only posted videos and pictures that they believed would help the court case, but also were involved in putting pressure on the city and FBI to continue investigating the case. They even had massive protests outside the courthouse on the day the young men went to trial and were convicted (Anderson, 2013). While it is unclear what Anonymous's ultimate contribution was in the outcome of the Steubenville trial, in Maryville, Missouri another rape case has been reopened due to their insistence (McGlensy, 2013). Like similar rape cases, in Maryville the girl was harassed, bullied, and her family even eventually left town only to see their unsold house burned (Diaz & Effron, 2014; Cowan, 2014). Anonymous put pressure on police and media to reopen the case, and in October 2013, after an article was published about the city and the case, a Grand Jury hearing was scheduled to see if the case should be reopened. Anonymous rejoiced.

Despite these signs that trolling ad-hocs can perform positive actions, in general, they are difficult to control and predict. A broader look at why this is follows.

More Is Different: Anonymous and MMORPGs

Clay Shirky, in his latest book *Cognitive Surplus* (2010), notes:

> You can have a large group of users. You can have an active group of users. You can have a group of users all paying attention to the same thing. Pick two, because you can't have all three at the same time. (p. 202)

Larger groups of entities (human or otherwise) behave in ways that are different than those that individuals might follow.

In *Out of Control: The New Biology of Machines, Social Systems, and the Economic World*, Kevin Kelly (1994) identified that networks of entities responded more like biological organisms—he calls them "vivisystems" or "hive minds," and calls nature an idea factory—or a "meme bank" (p. 3). Kelly writes that what makes the "hive mind" or ad-hoc special is that no one is in control and yet there is a certain amount of governance that emerges. In vivisystems, he states that lower-level individuals (in terms of the system not their own intelligence or biological complexity) in a group's behavior cannot predict the behavior of the swarm or ad-hoc as a whole. New patterns emerge when the bug becomes a swarm—and no computer today can completely predict how that works.

In MMORPGs (Massive Multiplayer Online Role Playing Games) groups of people will form guilds, dungeon parties, and raid groups not only because it is required by the game system to defeat bigger bosses, but because being part of such a group is fun (and offers a different kind of fun than solo play). Such groups assure that the guild will continue to be successful even if individuals leave, and enable types of play not available to individuals.

The primary difference between groups in MMORPGs and ad-hoc-racies outside of them is leadership. Many guilds have singular leaders—often the person that created the guild in the first place. MMORPGs also feature pick-up-groups (called PUGs) that individuals wanting to play with a group outside their guild can join. These are more similar to ad-hocs (indeed, some games refer to them as ad-hoc groups), but they are not always large enough for hive or swarm behavior to emerge. They also don't last long and individuals are likely to just play a pre-assigned role (such as doing damage or healing) for the group. Because group members know their part, they might not even have to commu-nicate, which leaves little room for creativity and even getting to know one another. Of course, anons don't really know one another either, so the primary limiting factor is the software (which breaks the group up if they do not immediately run through another dungeon or raid) and the nature of the task assigned. If no communication is needed, chances are the individuals will not want to work together again.

A swarming hive mind (or ad-hoc), on the other hand, does stay to-gether long enough to form its own patterns and not simply follow those laid out for it. According to Kelly (1994), hive minds have their own sort of internal logic and memory. This memory is distributed across many members. In this way, no single member's leaving can cause the memory of the group to fall apart. Computers can distribute memory across many different hard drives so that the loss of any single one does not cause the loss of as much data. Processing, too, can be done across a group of computers or people. 4Chan's groupthink is founded upon this memory, as is the lexicon that has grown for trolling.

With communication and time, groups can become even better at distributed memory and processing. In science, writes Kelly,

> It has long been appreciated . . . that large numbers behave differently than small numbers. Mobs breed a requisite measure of complexity for emergent entities. The total number of possible interactions between two or more members accumulates exponentially as the number of members increases. At a high level of connectivity, and a high number of members, the dynamics of mobs takes hold. More *is* different. (1994, p. 20)

Ad-Hocs lack centralized control—which means that they may end up moving in directions that their original members did not intend. They are highly adaptable and evolvable, as well as resilient and boundless (Kelly, 1994). They allow for very swift meme development as well as easy language adoption. On Reddit, for example, an odd turn of phrase in one sub-forum (called a subreddit) will easily be picked up by others. Some stories become "viral," at least on that site, very quickly. The ad-hoc can shift focus rapidly, and even if one person cannot wield it like a weapon certainly *enough* people online can direct their attention. Furthermore, even if Anonymous cannot be directed by one person, other ad-hocs can be. People who have adjusted themselves to being part of the mob are generally ready and willing to jump on a new one. Thus started GamerGate—when a man posted a long diatribe against his ex-girlfriend, accusing her of cheating and sleeping with someone for a positive game review, and started a now over year-long raid against women and feminists in gaming and (sometimes) game journalism.

However, in both cases discussed here (first against feminists and then *for* rape victims—which is not quite the same thing as being for feminists but is close), all "Rules" of the game created by the Rules of the Internet were kept. If we view the Internet through a lens of gaming, it is not one game with one enemy. The same people are not always good and not always bad. Gaming can be used to analyze and rethink many different situations—not just those wherein the ad-hoc is on the offense. In one game you are Mario fighting Bowser to save the Princess, and in the next you play Bowser driving a go-kart throwing a blue shell at the Princess. Your identity is changeable, the game is changeable, and it doesn't have to make complete sense as to why.

More Is Different: Theoretical Approaches. The power of organized numbers to both increase and decrease agency has been recognized in past years. In *Here Comes Everybody* (2008), Clay Shirky notes that ad-hoc-racies allow ordinary people to economically create large-scale changes and productions that were not available to them before. Thus, we witness individuals and groups able to organize in new and interesting ways. In fact, this claim is also made in *Wikinomics* (Tapscott & Williams, 2008) and in Kevin Kelley's *New Rules for the New Economy* (1998). The power of ad-hocracy has become popular in both high theory and business theory.

But the ad-hoc lingers elsewhere in critical theory pertaining to power and manipulation as well. Jeffrey Nealon (2007), in writing about the dividing line between Foucaultian discipline and biopower, notes that "as societies of control *extend* and *intensify* the tactics of discipline and biopower (by linking training and surveillance to ever-more-minute realms of everyday life), they also give birth to a whole new form. And this emergence comes about through what Foucault calls a 'swarming [l'essaimage] of disciplinary mechanisms,' through the intensification of discipline rather than its exhaustion or dissipation" (2007, p. 68). Foucault too, it seems, recognized the power of the "swarm" years before it became popular to discuss how numbers affect power. Hardt and Negri draw out the connections of power in groups to note that the "normalizing apparatuses of disciplinarity that internally animate our common and daily practices, but in contrast to discipline, this control extends well outside the structured sites of social institutions through flexible and fluctuating networks" (as cited in Nealon, 2007, pp. 68–69). Nealon argues that suggesting that the way that imperial or disciplinary power ends (by intensifying and turning into another form of power—biopower or control) is a very Foucaultian move. While I would agree, I also would argue that it is a move that also reflects the intensified nature of power within ad-hocracy.

Phillips (2015) recognizes that the power of these groups comes from their open and anonymous nature. When noting that some people want to stop antisocial trolling behavior online and suggest that we do so by walling off code and trying to prevent hacking and trolling if at all possible, she contends that in advocating this strategy we also "all but invite panoptic surveillance" and that these "pastures may be safer, but they are by no means green" (Phillips, 2015, p. 237). She goes on to say that:

> the same Internet that provides the space and freedom for people to make jokes about Over 9000 Penises and post incendiary comments on dead strangers' Facebook pages also provides

the space and freedom for people to organize, communicate securely, bypass oppressive censorship measures, and safely expose government corruption. Trolling may be an unpleasant side effect of such openness, but closing that which is open and naming that which is nameless risks creating far more problems than it would solve, particularly for those users who rely on online anonymity for reasons of political or personal safety. Attempt to smoke out the trolls, in other words, and you simultaneously smoke out the activists. (Phillips, 2015, p. 155)

However, other theorists argue that ad-hoc anonymity is less important than prevailing group structure. S. Alexander Haslam (2012) argues that tyranny and evil do not come from anonymity (as might have been proven by the Milgram experiment, which Phillips somewhat debunks), but instead might have more to do with identification with the authority in charge of a group and feeling that an authority is right. In an ad-hoc with no clear authority, then that feeling must be directed that the *group* is right—is it little wonder that these are often referred to as the "hivemind?" Haslam (2012) notes that if the group is normed to be destructive, then anonymity will make it more destructive. However, if the group is normed to be constructive, or slowly—over time—becomes constructive, as Anonymous has, then the anonymity of the group will make it *more* constructive.

It may even be possible that the ad-hoc was predicted by Marx himself. The ad-hoc can be considered just a new form of work group—perhaps an intensified one. Nealon notes that when the machine is introduced, a new kind of labor is also introduced alongside it. Would it not also stand to a certain sort of reason that with the introduction of the computer, that a new form of labor would also be introduced (and following Nealon's logic, as I do below, that new kind of labor should be intensified and restructured)?

> With the advent of the machine arrives a new kind of labor, no longer housed in the negating power of the individual worker (the labor theory of value), but distributed, machinelike, throughout the socius. This new "virtual" or distributed labor "does *not* exist in the worker's consciousness, but rather *acts upon him through the machine*. . . . Labor appears . . . scattered among the individual living workers at numerous points in a mechanical system; subsumed under the total process of the machinery itself, as itself

> only a link in the system, *whose unity exists not in the living work-*
> *ers, but rather in the living* (active) *machinery which confronts his*
> *individual.'* (Nealon, 2007, p. 83)

Machines in general require many workers that are distributed throughout the system to keep them running. Computer networks actually demand many more, though not perhaps in the ways that the economists
would wish. It takes many thousands of individuals to keep Wikipedia
up to date, for example, and these individuals are an ad-hoc. Nealon
notes that as we move into a new form of control (biopower), work extends to our daily lives and follows us everywhere. We check our e-mail
at home, we work on websites for free, we discuss race and create critical
race theory again and again on web forums when we challenge one another about privilege and entitlements, and we update articles on Wikipedia without a single person telling us that we have to do these things:

> Following the intense saturation of biopower's concepts and
> practices within everyday life, contemporary capitalism has *not*
> gone about setting *boundaries* on work, but rather has sought
> to *increase* works' saturation into the very fiber of everyday life.
> Think of yourself at home, answering e-mail at midnight. A
> highly intensified mode of biopower, then, is what one might
> call the 'operating' system of contemporary economic and cul-
> tural life. (Nealon, 2007, p. 85)

The ad-hoc of Wikipedia, the ad-hoc of a messageboard community, the
ad-hocs created by free journaling sites like Tumblr—this is some of the
work that saturates our daily life. But are these things that saturate our
daily lives work or play?

In his book *Communication Power* (2009), Manuel Castells calls ad-
hocs "network enterprises," noting that these groups seem to take place
from within networks: "Large corporations, and their subsidiary networks, usually form networks of cooperation, called, in business practice, strategic alliances or partnerships" (2009, p. 32). Because the ad-hoc
is rarely a permanent group, no matter who you look to for the definition, Castells fails to see them as a network in themselves. They are part
of a larger system, always, in his writing. They "link up on specific business projects, and reconfigure their cooperation in different networks
with each new project" (p. 32). They drift in and out of reality based
upon a given "product, process, time and space" (p. 32). It is most important that the network enterprise share information and knowledge,

not capital and labor, for Castells. However, because he sees this is a process that primarily happens in corporations (or in groups that could be described as corporate-like enterprises at the very least), he sees them first and foremost as part of a larger firm that is important for its capital accumulation. His "dominant layer" in the network is the global financial market. Although I suppose it could be argued otherwise, very few people believe that Wikipedia's importance lies within the global capital market—though its servers demand money and upkeep. Its value is in the sheer knowledge stored at the site, and even that is held in contempt for the way it was put there in the first place.

In any case, to simplify, I will use the term *ad-hocracy* to describe any distributed network socially-constructed around some sort of non-required task. Any individual member of an ad-hocracy is more likely to have a sustained presence online and actually meet their individual goals than a single individual who is attacked by one, as being a member of a collective group provides protection from the procedural rhetorics of other groups.

AD-HOCS AND ETHICS

Not that it should not be, but *fun* is certainly a goal of many Internet ad-hocs. As one of the largest, members of 4Chan say that the Internet should not be used for anything serious at all—that it is best for humor, gags, and quick dissemination of memes. 4Chan and those that follow them often quote a single line: "The Internet is serious business," which is also one of the rules of the Internet (2013). However, in so saying this they do not mean that everything on the Internet should be taken seriously. Instead they mean that other people interpret things that they find online far too seriously.

Because of their lack of seriousness, they are often judged as *only* a negative presence (not very surprisingly). Judging groups associated with new technologies as well as the technologies themselves as "good" or "bad" is a practice with a long history. It seems important to align ourselves along with the good and leave the bad to rot on their own. Even I am guilty of this practice, having joked that there are technologies that never belong in classrooms—like Chat Roulette. Overall, however, I do not see digital media and its users as being so simple to describe. There might well be things to learn from the so-called "bad" groups: ways of surviving online, learning new ways of arguing, and not leaving the "bad" out of the larger cultural story of how we argue online at any given time. Janet Murray (2006), for example, is more interested in "cyberdrama" than value judgment. According to Murray:

> The question that most often arises, in one form or another, in "new media" practice, is how do we tell a good one from a bad one? . . . But the more useful question is, how do we make a better cyberdrama? One criterion that I have found useful is the concept of dramatic agency. Agency is the term I use to distinguish the pressure of interactivity, which arises from the two properties of the procedural and the participatory. When the world responds expressively and coherently to our engagement with it, then we experience agency. (2006, p. 10)

Rather, then, than arguing that any given ad-hoc (like Anonymous) is a purely good or bad presence online, I would like to look at how they affect the Internet and affect the agency of themselves and others through organized numbers and procedural rhetorics.

The Development of Anonymous and Other Ad-hocs

Scientology. In 2007 it would have been easy to argue that the day's digital ad-hocs were nearly all working towards negative ends and that socially positive ad-hocs needed to be formed to work against them. However, as mentioned earlier, every year since that time has seen more positive raids that get major media attention. One of the most famous of such "good" instances is Anonymous's 2008–2009 raid on the Church of Scientology (CoS), providing, of course, that you are not a member of the Church. They based their attack on three points: (1) Scientology charges people lots of money to belong to what Anonymous called a "cult," (2) the censorship of a video by Tom Cruise describing Scientology meant for other Scientologists from YouTube, and (3) the eventual forced suicide of a Church of Scientology member (PartyVan Wiki, 2011). Anonymous began a worldwide campaign to make sure that the website for the CoS was dropped, that sensitive Church documents meant only for members were leaked to the general public online (a move popularized later on by WikiLeaks), and that various offices would receive many pizzas, free shipping boxes, and be serenaded by the voice of Rick Astley each time they picked up their phone (Encyclopedia Dramatica, 2010).

In the years between the "Feminazi" wars and these cases (2012 and 2013), Anonymous's vigilante justice had been aimed at progressively bigger and more powerful targets. They carried out "raids" and harassment on the RIAA (after several high-profile documented cases of people being sued for millions if not billions of dollars for downloading music and movies), a few sites that had stolen ideas from 4Chan and turned them profitable, and the Church of Scientology. "Project Chanology," as the Church of Scientology (CoS) raid was called, was about changing the public's perception of the Church and hopefully increasing people's mindfulness of it. Although the censorship (by the Church of Scientology) of a video featuring Tom Cruise was one of the reasons this particular raid started, it was also timely—*South Park* had featured an episode describing the beliefs of the Church of Scientology with the words "This is what Scientologists really believe" (Parker, 2005) at the bottom that had been highly controversial and had led to the actor that provided the voice of Chef to leave the show under duress.

Because Anonymous was, for perhaps the first time, attacking a target that other people were currently working against, a man by the name of Mark Bunker from XenuTV created a YouTube video telling Anonymous that while he was behind what they were doing, he recommended that they only used legal methods to attack the Church (Encyclopedia Dramatica, 2010). While most people who have directly addressed Anonymous in this way have become targets themselves, Bunker was able to get Anonymous's attention because of his true devotion to being anti-CoS (Church of Scientology), and the group transformed. He recommended that they peacefully protest and push for governments around the world to remove the Church's tax-exempt status. It is noted on Encyclopedia Dramatica that the success of the peaceful rallies held around Church of Scientology buildings on February 10 and March 15 of the following year by people wearing Guy Fawkes' masks was potentially because of Bunker's help (2010). He is now sometimes even referred to as the "Wise Beard Man."

Although the Church of Scientology still exists, Anonymous had many successes over them including anti-CoS media coverage on Fox News, in *Wired*, and in *Maxim*; nearly all "top-secret" documents from the Church being made publicly available online; some missions and organizations have closed; Rick Astley complimented them on their use of his music; the LAPD dropped all charges against one of the members of Anonymous and began investigating the Church instead; and more

Scientology front groups have been exposed (Encyclopedia Dramatica, Project Chanology, 2010). One of the goals of this "game" was to expose beliefs that Anonymous thought were ridiculous and to educate the public about what the Church of Scientology believes—an act that was started by *South Park*. Given those goals, the raid was successful.

Since the attacks on the Church of Scientology, Anonymous has also been involved in tracking down pedophiles and helping authorities find a young girl who videotaped herself throwing puppies into a river and laughing about it. More recently, they have been involved in keeping WikiLeaks solvent, while publishing articles about companies that have cancelled people's accounts due to WikiLeaks donations such as Visa and MasterCard.

Project Backtrace. Anonymous has not entirely stopped their raids on individuals and smaller sites—though most of those raids now are carried on by 4Chan; however, many of the smaller targets they do have are "personal" to the group. For example, after being involved in Project Chanology, Jennifer Emick left Anonymous and began her own private Internet security firm called "Project Backtrace" (Biddle, 2012). She seeks out the real names and addresses of various Anonymous members and reports them to the FBI for illegal activity. Naturally this made her an ideal target for the group. Her side of the story is that she left Anonymous when their activities became illegal rather than legal, peaceful protests. However, Anonymous always used some illegal activity in their raids. For example, Denial of Service attacks on networked servers are not legal.

Other Potential Issues. In light of the rape cases that Anonymous has become involved in, there are some people who are concerned that their illegal actions will ultimately cause harm to someone—if not to themselves, then to one of the people they are trying to protect. Online feminists posting at popular sites like Feministe and Jezebel have come forward both in support of Anonymous's current actions but also worried about their ultimate outcome (Filopovic, 2013; Caldwell, 2013; Dries, 2013). If illegal means are used to find evidence, that evidence might not be permissible in court, for example, meaning that victims may not ultimately earn justice from the US court system. If the wrong person is "doxxed" in relation to a crime, their reputation could be damaged forever. When the Boston Marathon bombings happened, Reddit used its millions of members to attempt to go over video and pictures taken at the scene to find the perpetrator. The person they identified was not the person who set the bomb. Later, Internet ad-hocs related to both Anonymous and Reddit were involved in harassing a man by the same name as the bomber—sometimes the hive mind finds the wrong person, and it is difficult to recover from their attacks even if a person is completely innocent. The methods of persuasion that these ad-hocs use, being essentially fallacious, can be deeply harmful if misdirected.

Anonymous proves that ad-hocs really can develop and change direction, even without a figurehead leader. They grew out of

> the witty, inventive, bilious and gleefully misogynistic message boards of the website 4chan. It grew out of one sub-scene in particular, the anything goes /b/ board, a place where rape didn't denote a crime but a commonplace suffix; a shorthand, alongside "nigger" and "fag" for the chan culture's hostility to the idea that anything could be offensive or go too far. Celebrated rituals on the site involved bullying, and stalking teenage girls and tricking minors into taking naked photos of themselves, which would then be posted and passed around online. (Siegel, 2013)

As Jacob Siegel notes in an article about Anonymous's taking on various rape cases for *The Daily Beast* (2013), 4Chan in its earliest stages was creative but vicious. On one hand they were creating memes used in many other online venues, but they also were inscrutable, goofy, and marginalized. It was very easy to spend time online and ignore that 4Chan existed (or never hear of it at all). But somewhere along the way, probably in or around Project Chanology, Anonymous and 4Chan began to understand the power that they had, not over individuals, but over the whole of the English-speaking Internet (at the very least). They are able to set an agenda for issues that are important to the world at large, and Siegel argues that since that time they have been moving towards becoming a "mainstream anti-establishment culture" and taking on cases that its older group would have decimated (Siegel, 2013, para. 6).

Despite their more "serious" focus, they have not lost the ability to create memes and quickly disseminate information. They create online cultural icons much as they did in the past, and retain their lack of structure. Their ability in invention and discovery is nearly unparalleled online as well, though the materials they create are not drawn from classical rhetoric either. To further examine how these groups create social and digital change, I will next define their rhetoric as procedural.

3 Defining the Internet as a Game

None of the aforementioned writers in chapter 1 or 2 take the step of showing how gaming rhetoric seeps into digital rhetoric and that by using gaming logic, numbers, and anonymity users can become more empowered in arguing rhetorically online. In order to define gaming as a lens to view Internet arguments, I will consider the work of McKenzie Wark and Jesper Juul alongside Ian Bogost.

In *Gamer Theory* (2007), McKenzie Wark—also author of *The Hacker Manifesto* (2005)—considers *gamespace*, a far-reaching term that describes the way we conceive of the spaces in which we work, live, and play. *Gamespace* is not just a word applied to virtual worlds, but is instead applied to all sorts of spaces. Gamespace is compared to a (post)modern-day Plato's Cave wherein the reflection of the game both is and becomes our culture. By living in a world dominated by games and game-language, we begin to see our entire world as one of winners and losers—and games abound. When you conceptualize that society is dominated by the idea that all of our lives are governed by games, it becomes more possible to start considering the effects of games in non-gamic spaces (such as the Internet or classrooms).

One of the primary arguments of games studies' past is about narratology. Most concisely: theorists argue whether or not games need to have stories, or whether or not games even *can* tell a story since different players play them in different ways. This is important for our purposes because arguments online and trolling often involve the rewriting of narrative: telling a new story—true or not—about another Internet user, or rewriting the worst form of their argument and arguing against it instead, and it is also important because considering narrative is thus necessary to defining *game* in the first place. Jesper Juul (2005) argues that games are both rules and fiction, rather than one or the other. We tell a fiction about a game, and create it through playing as well. Games are fun because they are interactive and because the rules create an adequate space for gameplay. Juul repeatedly quotes and paraphrases Sid Meier, creator and game designer of *Civilization*, in saying that "a game is a series of interesting choices" (2005, p. 19). Choices create mental challenges for players, and as Jane McGonigal (2011) and James Paul Gee (2003) argue, people like challenges. There are certain kinds of work that we enjoy, and certain kinds of challenges that we seek out (McGonigal, 2011). We spend hours trying to beat our friends and colleagues in *Candy Crush Saga* on Facebook, for example, while many people dislike their jobs and school. McGonigal seeks to harness our energy for gaming into social good, while I would like to harness procedural rhetorics for social good. In the Internet as a game, the Internet becomes a place of challenges as well. Different rules create different games, and looking at the Internet as a game does not mean that there is one, singular, game that can be read from it.

In *Half-Real,* one of the studies that Jesper Juul (2005) examines was done by Linda Hughes and examines how a group of girls played Foursquare, a playground game using a ball and chalked square. Their use of the rules varies: Foursquare

> turns out to be a combination of official and unofficial rules, conflicting success criteria, and rule negotiation. According to Hughes, "Game rules can be interpreted and interpreted toward preferred meanings and purposed, selectively invoked or ignored, challenged or defined, changed or enforced to suit the collective goals of different groups of players. In short, players can take the same game and collectively make of it strikingly difference experience" (1999, 94). This is a convincing argument, and part of the larger point that children's games cannot be meaningfully described only as the rules that make them up. (Juul, 2005, p. 11)

The girls would talk about the rules, and rules varied from one age group of girls to another. The rules developed over time as well, and most players were aware that the rules in use now were not the rules used a few years ago. However, Juul notes that some theorists want to take this to its logical extreme and say that rules don't matter at all. Since rules are negotiable this means that they could be almost anything, the girls could be doing anything else instead of Foursquare but still are calling it Foursquare. However,

> a more detailed analysis of Foursquare reveals that the protracted structure of the game, with no clear termination, no final winner, and no clear score count *allows* the players to play while

having many other considerations than simply perfecting their own performance. Moreover, the unclearness of some rules such as the rule against slamming makes room for all kinds of social power play. At the same time, the players have *chosen* to play this game rather than other games, and players change the rules because they want to play *this game*, with specific rules. We cannot ignore the role of the rules without ignoring a basic aspect of the player experience: that different games yield different kinds of experiences. (2005, p. 12)

People choose to play by certain rules, or participate in a certain game despite its rules, as there are nearly always rules that a player does not like, such as those that make it challenging or losable.

According to Juul,

Video games are two different things at the same time: video games are *real* in that they consist of real rules with which players actually interact, and in that winning or losing a game is a real event. However, when winning a game by slaying a dragon, the dragon is not a real dragon but a fictional one. To play a video game is therefore to interact with real rules while imagining a fictional world, and a video game is a set of rules as well as a fictional world. (2005, p. 1)

The thing is—when you are fighting against a person online, they seem just as fantastic as that dragon. The group you are with feels real—just as real as joining in a group to play a dungeon or a raid in an MMORPG does. But the other person that is targeted by the ad-hoc group? They have to be demonized for the frothy mob to form. An essential part of forming an ad-hoc becomes coming up with something for the ad-hoc to do, gathering people who want to do it in the way you want it done, and forming up a fiction as a group that makes your actions sensible. But how is that a game (other than the metaphor used by Anonymous and 4Chan of a "raid," that is)?

From the discussion of games as rules, fiction, narrative, players, etc. Juul (2005) wrote a basic definition of a game that has six basic features:

1. Rules—Games are rule based.
2. Games have variable, quantifiable outcomes.

3. Valorization of outcome: The different potential outcomes of the game are assigned different values, some positive and some negative.

4. Player effort: the player exerts effort in order to influence the outcome (games are challenging).

5. Player attached to outcome: the player is emotionally attached to the outcome of the game in the sense that player will be a winner and "happy" in case of a positive outcomes, but a loser and 'unhappy' in case of a negative outcome.

6. Negotiable consequences: the same game [set of rules] can be played with or without real world consequences. (Juul, 2005, p. 36)

In short, Juul defines a game as "a rule-based system with a variable and quantifiable outcome, where different outcomes are assigned different values, the player exerts effort in order to influence the outcome, the player feels emotionally attached to the outcome, and the consequence of the activity are negotiable" (2005, p. 36).

To view the Internet as a game (according to Juul's definition), then, we should examine which parts of this definition can be applied to Internet arguments.

GAMES ARE RULE-BASED

First, most Internet communities feature a number of rules, some of which lend themselves toward play and some of which do not. These rules are culturally constructed by individual sites or groups of sites. Rules might be posted, unstated, or both. A group mentioned before (4Chan) even has written a list of humorous rules called Rules of the Internet that include things such as Rule 34: "If it exists, there is porn of it" (2013). These rules can be used to create a game of sorts on their own. Following he Rules of the Internet, an individual would be required to understand that all arguments can be dismissed and that anything nameable can also be hated (Rules of the Internet, 2013).

Additionally, while some of the rules are written down in the (now defunct or at least abandoned) PartyVan Wiki on an actual list called the Rules of the Internet, other rules of trolling as a subculture are implied and culturally ingrained. You are made fun of for being new (a "newfag") until you understand them, and even then you might get made fun of for being an "oldfag." You have to understand that such terms are not to be taken at face value—they are used against everyone equally. Of course, depending on their sexuality and empathy, some people will be more bothered by the term than others. Furthermore, some of the unwritten rules—such as "everyone here makes rape jokes"—means that some of the trolls that Phillips (2015) interviewed admit to being female and loving to go online and write rape jokes. It might seem like chaos, but a very strict system of rules with its own lexicon, memes, and history governs this behavior. Another group of "players" of this game could easily have their own; for example, the Alt-Right trolls *do* seem to believe the sexist and racist things that they post, so while they build their community upon many of the same memes, they do not play with quite the same trickster voice as the others.

It is necessary to note here the difference between "rules" and "procedures." The rules of these organizations set up the culture, their goals, their attitudes, where the "game" happens, and the way that it happens. The rules suggest that this game is not fair, that everyone online is subject to it, and that it is a little ridiculous. They essentially state: "if you treat the Internet seriously and argue badly on it, bad things could happen to you." The procedures—the way that people have proceduralized online argument into easy lists of things to do—are not the same things as rules. As such, these procedures are largely written about on their own later in this text. Some of the most popular procedures (like memes and the use of certain terms) also appear in the rules, but each individual raid will have its own procedures that are best suited for that rhetorical purpose.

VARIABLE AND QUANTIFIABLE OUTCOMES

There also must be variable and quantifiable outcomes. In other words, if a game always has the same result or winning condition, it is not really a game, or if the outcome is randomized, it is gambling and not actually a game. As such, the outcome of Internet arguments that I look at must be ultimately variable (either party could "win"), and there must be some rules or quantification that counts as "winning." Winning is often a matter of simply continuing to exist—not being silenced. It also means that the person who is arguing has to want to win, and must have a "winning condition" in mind, whether that be simply overwhelming the other person's argument, silencing them, getting them to delete their account, or simply angering them. Unlike many other forms of rhetoric, this type of procedural rhetoric found in online communities often calls for the *audience* to determine the outcome of the game.

Valorization of Outcome

The final outcome of the game must also be valorized—winning is good, losing is bad. Shutting down one's site should be considered to be bad, while continuing to operate and even gaining an audience after a "fight" should be good. If the attacking ad-hoc is fighting for the minority groups that I will study (instead of against them—sadly more common), then the shutdown of hate sites or silencing of bigots would be considered a valorous outcome. More recently (as of 2015), Anonymous has been working diligently to shut down pro-ISIS sites as well.

According to Phillips, trolls privilege logic over emotion, which feeds into their obsession with winning as well. She states that trolls define winning as "successfully exerting dominance over a given adversary" (2015, p. 124). She notes that their argumentative style follows the adversary method that Janice Moulton theorized as the defining feature of Western philosophy. The adversary method sets up the ground rules for the way that "proper" argumentation works and "presupposes the superiority of male-gendered traits (rationality, assertiveness, dominance) over female-gendered traits (sentimentality, cooperation, conciliation). In the process, it privileges and in fact reifies an explicitly androcentric worldview while simultaneously delegitimizing less confrontational discursive modes" (Phillips, 2015, p. 124). Winning, then, might be defined by the audience of trolls in a completely different way than by the feminists they are trolling. Without an agreed-upon, set, winning condition, it is difficult for trolled individuals and groups to see trolling for the game that it is, even if they do understand the concept of lulz.

Player Effort

All of this, of course, takes effort—often many hours are spent defending a site, creating arguments, making infographics and memes, raising awareness, and organizing an ad-hoc. On 4Chan, people plan a raid quickly but have to keep up their efforts since posts are deleted automatically when they move off the main page. Authors like Sweeney (2013) and other anti-trolls have spent hundreds of hours in the past years attempting to silence trolls and even have some arrested. While physical effort is not expended (at least not usually more than a video game), no one can say that it does not take player effort to win one of these arguments. Furthermore, players are very attached to the outcome. Although not everyone is as emotional as Sweeney is about RIP Trolls, most digital rhetoricians do care about winning fights or not. Our tendency to take such arguments far too seriously has even been memorialized in memes and comics.

CONSEQUENCES ARE NEGOTIABLE

Lastly, although it will not be immediately clear, there are negotiable consequences to playing the Internet as if it were a game. Though some actions are illegal and therefore legally actionable, most consequences of online rhetorical play are ultimately left to the audience to determine. In this way, the role of the audience cannot be ignored in determining the "winner" of digital arguments. In some cases, procedural rhetoric allows for the audience to determine the "winning condition."

DEFINITION

The Internet of massive anonymous ad-hocracies can be viewed as a game because there are rules guiding interaction on it (do this not that) that lead to variable and quantifiable outcomes, where outcomes are assigned different values, players exert effort to influence those outcomes, players become emotionally attached to the outcomes, and most of the consequences of the activity online are negotiable. People can *choose*, however, to take those consequences into real world situations, which they increasingly do both for better and for worse. Some procedurally rhetorical moves *nearly always* have real-life consequences, such as doxxing and "swatting" (the process of sending police to a target's home on a false tip reporting them for drug or other illegal activity), but most are more negotiable with virtual effects rather than physical ones. Players follow set procedures that are used to mobilize groups in the game, which enable the massive amounts of players to function as singular entities.

More specifically, we can view the Internet through the lens of gaming by noting that:

1. Rules: The Internet can be viewed through culturally-constructed as well as written rules.

2. Variable, quantifiable outcomes: The Internet, as a game, can have no consequences or many. Sites can be shut down, lives destroyed, or what occurs on it can have no bearing in real life at all. The participants set the stakes. The rules clearly lay out a winning condition, so it is possible to quantify any outcome. However, part of that quantification is in the eye of the rhetorical audience. Both parties can feel themselves to be the winner. Often, if a losing condition is met by game players they will simply choose to play until a winning condition is met when the other person quits.

3. Valorization of outcome: People fight to win—simply. Shutting down a site is seen as positive for one group while education might be the goal of another.

4. Player effort: Players on both sides of any online conflict put significant effort into their posts, flame wars, and denial of service attacks as well as their rhetoric—traditional, visual, and procedural. Most players put hours into any given argument.

5. Player attached to outcome: Although groups may declare that the Internet is not meant for serious business, those same groups can be motivated to great political effect and, in fact, use the Internet for serious business when they care about the outcome of a fight.

6. Negotiable consequences: In this case, the Internet as a game is sometimes played with real world consequences and sometimes not. Between 2015–2017, many ad-hocs took on a political slant—either extremely conservative or extremely liberal—with serious effects to real world politics.

Thus, the Internet can be described as a game theoretically, or viewed through a lens of gaming, which allows the Internet to be examined for rhetorics beyond traditional kinds, including procedural rhetoric.

Juul—specifically—is useful in building this definition because he notes that games are not tied "to any specific medium or any media: card games are played on computers, sports continue to be a popular video game genre, and video games occasionally become board games" (2005, p. 48). Other theorists are more specific about the medium of a game, but to Juul a game might be a sport, a console cartridge, a video game, a board game, a playground game—or, I would argue, an argument.

PRESENCE AND IDENTITY IN THE GAME OF THE INTERNET

Considering the Internet through the lens of gaming changes more than the types of rhetoric (such as procedural) that might be a part of it. One way that the play-element of games changes rhetoric is that it changes the way we discuss our own presence in them. For example, when we insult someone and say they are a bitch (Ana Marjanovic-Shane's example is a pig) it really is just a metaphor meant to cast the received in a negative light—unless, of course, they have reclaimed *bitch* in a positive manner. However, in a game, saying that someone is a bitch (or a pig) might well transform them into that animal beyond the metaphor. In a video game, your avatar might be physically transformed. In the Game of the Internet, the receiver of such an insult is not just being harassed, they are having the online narrative that they use to represent themselves rewritten (2007). Jesper Juul writes:

> . . . if we utter the sentence "Brian is a pig," this is usually considered a metaphor and an insult. A metaphor, since we would propose a transfer our ideas of a pig to Brian as a person, and an insult, since this would cast Brian in a negative light. But as Ana Marjanovic-Shane describes, to say, "Brian is a pig" while playing a game does not describe Brian as a person; it only says that in this play context, Brian assumes the role of a pig. (2007, p. 11)

Does this mean that people don't hold the same culpability for the things they say in games or online? Or should we hold more culpability because we have the power to transform their online selves? Can we treat them as meaningless even if they still hurt the people they are aimed at? Juul goes on to note that Marjanovic-Shane says that "Brian is a pig" *literally* only survives upon the "fictive plane," and that this has little to do with reality. Actions in a game have multiple realities—you roll dice and this lets you know if you have the power, at the moment, to attack and defeat a foe. You defeat someone in a game but not in real life. Thus, you have a real identity, a virtual one, and a projected one (Gee, 2003).

Does "I bet she's fat" really mean "I bet she's fat?" or does it mean the writer has been culturally conditioned to think that this is something to say to make someone feel bad without it being true, or both at the same time? Does it actually transform the mental image the audience of such an insult has of the person it is about? This all happens on the "fictive plane" (Juul, 2005). Your presence is changed in the game to a pig or an enemy or a bombshell—at least to everyone else playing. The problem is that for many women, especially, it does change their real-world perception or mirrors things they have been told culturally or in real life. Trolls count on people taking their insults seriously and enjoy it when they do. If the recipient does not take on the identity (does not take the identity seriously), then the troll cannot generate lulz from it.

When the game is in play, we enter into a new space—something that Jeffery Nealon (2005) refers to as the *biopolitical realm* in his own examples, but one that I will simply refer to as "gamespace" after Wark (2007). Within this gamespace the personal and private can be affected by the ethics of the majority—which might be far different from the ethics of the individual. Within this, both the groups attacking others and those that are often on the defensive, such as feminists, find themselves considering and reconsidering. When you play a game, you are more in the game than in the real world. When you move your hand, you are moving your hand in real space, but you are also making the Rabbids collect trash to get to the moon or the Prince make a better Katamari (Juul, 2005). When you tell someone that you wish they would be raped, you aren't just winning an argument via an *ad hominem* attack, you may also be affecting a feminist's sense of self or place in the world. Should we learn to resist this power over our real bodies through gamespace, should we learn to fight back, or should we learn to transform these stereotypical gamespaces into non-stereotypical ones?

If not all players know they are playing or that even the Internet could be viewed as gamic, this becomes unethical. Is it fair to play with people who don't know they are playing? Can we even begin to divide trolling that is play from trolling that is serious? The very *essence* of trolling calls for the person under attack to not get it. If they understand trolling, they are very unlikely to be able to be trolled. It is for this reason that I cannot define the Internet directly as a game—one cannot say the Internet *is* a game because not everyone playing knows the rules or knows that they are playing. However, using it as a lens to view certain conversations as game-like and rhetorical still is possible.

Internet Fame

A second key to understanding procedural rhetoric outside of video games is studying and understanding the power of mobs in digital environments, and understanding how these mobs predict and cause Internet fame. Much like interactions on MMORPGs, the actions of Internet ad-hocs, when properly organized, can do much more and much better work than any individual alone. The flexibility of the ad-hoc allows it to transform itself, transfer power, and recreate itself whenever necessary until the ultimate end of the conflict without "losing face." Most of the Internet-famous have gained their fame through procedural rhetoric— by following a known algorithm or formula (or being the one to create an algorithm or formula in some cases) that was easily reproducible and linkable while also being rhetorically effective. Memes could not spread quickly without being somewhat algorithmic and laid out by a strict set of procedures: (1) Take picture, (2) add text, and (3) profit. Meme creators do so through having an exploitable fault in their base material—Grumpy Cat looks grumpy, but also has dwarfism, for example. They also gain power through having a large audience and intuiting how to manipulate that audience and get the audience to work for them. People who like Grumpy Cat put new words on his pictures and repost him. The "Internet famous" creator of Grumpy Cat does not have to do as much work because that work is distributed to the fans.

Failure and Psychosocial Moratoria

As noted earlier, many people enjoy arguing online. If we take such arguments as a game, it can help us explain why (other than the explicit joy in telling someone else they are wrong). In some of his later writing, Jesper Juul (2013) has explored why we like failing in games. But wait—isn't the whole point of using procedural rhetorics to look at online arguments to expose their structure and therefore win? Well, perhaps. But in viewing them as games we can also look at failing in these arguments more like we fail in games and less like failing in school. I would also argue that we may be able to learn how to treat school failure as more like failing in games as well. In short, *we can learn to treat argument less like "serious business" and more like play.* Accountability can be lowered, in many instances, which would create a rhetorical condition similar to the "psychosocial moratorium principle" that Gee (2003) developed by looking at video games. If we can lower the social, cognitive, and real-world consequences of an action, we can encourage people to take that action much more easily. In online arguments, including trolling, this occurs. Trolling groups allow it to happen. Simon Penny notes:

> Pierre Bordieu (1977) and others have established that social behaviors are often learned without conscious behavioral understanding. The way someone rationalizes or explains an activity on an intellectual level, and the behaviors that have been learned and are enacted can be different, even diametrically opposed. There is a small industry of corporate training in the reading and deployment of body language. Legion are the training and rehabilitation systems which rely on repetitive physical action, even to exhaustion. From this perspective, military boot camp, football training, some forms of yoga and other spiritual training, ballet lessons, and some schools of drug, juvenile delinquency and other psychosocial rehabilitation are almost indistinguishable, except on the level of academicization of the particular techniques. (Penny, 2004, p. 74)

One of the ways that games change accountability is by their rules. Rules that make a person less accountable for his or her actions in a specific environment mean that people will behave as if their accountability is reduced.

Please note, however, that reduced accountability in online systems has always been, and will continue to be, an equally problematic feature of those systems. Online hate gives power to hate in the "real world." Many nations lack the laws, authority, and technical knowledge to prosecute hate and threats online, and so while reduced accountability can lead to creativity and experimentation, it can also lead to bullying and hate crimes. Hate online can be carried into the real world, and in the case of groups like ISIS, people can be trained in hate and terrorism directly online. Deindividuation is a serious concern, and should not be taken lightly. Neither should the influence of anonymous groups on real-world politics, such as one board on 4Chan's claims that they helped elect Trump by "elect[ing] a meme as President" (Ohlheiser, 2016).

In Juul's "The Art of Failure" (2013), he connects failure with art. In art, tragedies, and games, we want there to be a certain amount of unpleasantness. Without that unpleasantness the game, play, or piece of art feels less authentic. He also postulates, as does Gee (2003), that games create a safe space within which we can fail but also try again, and that creating places wherein we can fail but it is not unpleasant to do so is an important use of them. Only in games can we prevent our friends and acquaintances from reaching their goals without actually damaging that relationship. Games, according to Juul (2013), create an inadequacy in us and then give us a way to fix that inadequacy—by playing the game. Games have designers and writers that create experiences so that we will want to brush ourselves off from failure and try again—Internet communities are not explicitly designed that way. Perhaps they should be, but in the meantime learning about how procedural rhetorics shape our arguments online can help us develop new strategies for viewing and responding to failure.

In school, when you fail to persuade your teacher you ultimately fail the assignment (at least in writing class). Use a fallacy and you are assuring yourself a bad grade. But the same student can come home from class, use that fallacy, and "win" when their target shuts down their site or stops posting—it's hard to convince students that traditional rhetoric is the only way of arguing well when so-called "poor" arguments often win.

Other forms of fiction deal with unpleasantness and failure as well, but not quite in the way that games do. To look at arguments online as games, we are thus prepared for a certain amount of that failure. Fiction and movies tend to look at the fears, self-doubt, and failure of others, while games examine our own self-doubts, failures, and fears (Juul, 2013). Juul describes video games as a kind of "art of failure" in that games set us up for failure and allow us to experiment with and experience it in a safe setting (2013, loc. 467). The trolls are already experimenting—perhaps not with failure, perhaps with manipulation— but their targets and their defenders are far less likely to "play." In the absence of rhetorical play (and safety—no one should ever take death threats completely un-seriously), defenders do not have the opportunity to learn forms of argument likely to cause less failure or even ways to co-opt some rhetorical strategies for their own movements.

Procedurally rhetorical arguments (and the sites of study that I have chosen to represent them) will also prove that the audience for a piece of writing online is almost always *everyone*—digital rhetoric differs from traditional rhetoric in that its audience is very broad and can potentially be seen by many more and far different individuals than the rhetor originally intended. People rarely intend to make 4Chan or Anonymous angry—but when they do, the ad-hoc swarms. As time goes on, that is even true of more liberally-minded groups. When a marketing executive on a trip to Africa in 2014 made a racist post to Twitter while in an airport, she did not expect it to go beyond her 110 follows (Ronson, 2015). However, by the time her plane landed, thousands of people were calling for her to be fired and had messaged her personally using Twitter to let her know how little they appreciated her "joke" (it was about being white and the likelihood of her catching AIDS while in the country). We don't expect to bring on the angry mob—but we are vulnerable when we think we have a private audience but do not. In fact, in his book *So You've Been Publicly Shamed* (2015), Jon Ronson follows several examples of people who have come under online shamings not just by 4Chan and Anonymous but by what seems like the internet at large.

MEMES

Lastly, today's procedural online rhetorics are largely based upon short, pithy phrases and memes. Richard Dawkins (1976) defines the *meme* as a unit that carries cultural information that can be transmitted and replicated. Online, most memes are regarded as such when they go viral and spread quickly. Memes are one method of Internet argumentation that are gamic and appear in nearly every example because online arguments form them, and also because they are a building block of the community of ad-hocs that I study. Many of the most popular memes also started in communities like 4Chan, which makes their relationship to the studies contained in the rest of the book irrefutable.

By being unmoderated and allowing what could be referred to as "complete freedom of speech," 4Chan and sites like it have also been behind some of the most famous Internet memes ever created. For example, the first known reference to a "lolcat" was made in 2005 on 4Chan. Since that time, combining pictures of cats with poorly spelled *messages* (naturally, because cats can't spell) has become a huge online success, especially around people who have no idea where the term originated. Today, one can find many different versions of the original cats. The "Cheeseburger" network has sprung up that provides user-created lolcats and dogs, and my personal favorite loltheorists—which features jokes that play off of a good working knowledge of critical theory.

Lolcats are possibly one of the most famous memes that 4Chan ever created. They have garnered critical attention at academic conferences and even are worth a mention in Clay Shirky's *Cognitive Surplus* (2010). He describes them as being simply a "cute picture of a cat that is made even cuter by the addition of a cute caption, the ideal effect of 'cat plus caption' being to make the viewer laugh out loud" (Shirky, *Cognitive Surplus*, 2010, p. 17). Shirky also notes that lolcats are a kind of digital mashup, a "combination of existing materials into something new" as somebody "adds a caption to an existing picture" (2010, p. 86). People online are more likely to refer to these pictures as "macros" than "mash-ups."

Whatever you call them, Shirky describes these as the "stupidest possible creative act," (2010, p. 86). He seems to think their importance comes purely from their existence, while I believe that their power as a fast-spreading meme means they are significantly more useful and more powerful rhetorically than he acknowledges. In getting stuck talking about this form and the rules it follows, Shirky breaks his own rules about not viewing the technology as a technology first, and thus misses the memetic power of lolcats' original creators.

4Chan is known for spreading viral media and memes. 4Chan was also behind "Rick-rolling," the process of replacing a movie online with all or part of Rick Astley's "Never Gonna Give you Up" (1987), the most famous incidence of which occurred during the Thanksgiving Day Parade in 2008. Rick Astley himself appeared on the *Foster's Home for Imaginary Friends* float. While the characters were singing a different song, Astley emerged from a hidden spot, interrupted and sang his song, and then a costumed character from the show/float said, "I love rick-rolling!" (KnowYourMeme, 2011). 4Chan also made the new *My Little Pony: Friendship is Magic* (*MLP:FiM*) television series into a number of viral memes that have in turn recursively affected the show itself. 4Chan began naming the various background ponies (including "Derpy Pony," "Dr. Whooves/My Little Timelord," and a DJ they named "DJ Pon-3"), creating images using them, and generally using ponies to spam more than other memes. In a promotional video released by the Hub (the television station that the show was on at the time), DJ Pon-3 is directly mentioned (Hasbro, "Equestria Girls," 2011) and "Derpy," a pony with crossed eyes, was named directly in an episode by Rainbow Dash. For the show's one hundredth episode, all these background characters were given center stage for one episode. Despite the negative Web presence of 4Chan, the producers of *MLP: FiM* not only were able to see the good in the site and the fandom it spawned, but realized that their fan input could ultimately be used to increase viewership and sales. Going into the fifth season, *MLP: FiM* remains popular with adult men (Bronies) and continues to be supported by lots of fan content. This is the sort of action that I wish my classrooms could take—even if they did not directly influence a television show, there is no reason to presume they could not directly affect someone other than their classmates.

Christopher Poole, the creator of 4Chan, has been hailed by *Time Magazine* as the "Master of Memes," and the magazine described his site as "the wellspring from which a lot of Internet culture, and hence popular culture, bubbles" (Smith, 2008). Memes that are created on 4Chan may well die there, but many of them escape into the Internet at large. Even while a lot of content on 4Chan can be racist, sexist, homophobic, misogynistic, full of swear words, and packed with every other type of porn (Smith, 2008), it is also the hotbed of pure, unadulterated invention online, and I think that it is worth studying and worth emulating, to some extent.

THE POWER OF SINGULAR GROUP IDENTITIES

Anonymous (and other groups like it) has a major advantage over anyone that they might want to target because they hold a uniquely structured group identity. Each individual member generally will post with the same user identification when a raid or other attack is taking place. If a website allows them, this identity will often just be "anonymous" or whatever default username is given to unregistered users.

So why is this more powerful? Many users using the same (or similar) name allows them to seem very prolific and means that posts can be made (or DDoS attacks) at all times of the day.

It also means that while no single user has a lot of power within the group, the group itself is powerful, which gives each user posting under that name a lot of power. Rather than joining into a conversation as a person new to a conversation that is likely to be ignored for being a "n00b," a group using a single identity will be able to give that powerful identity to new users with important things to say who should be listened to. The group empowers the individual rhetorician.

When other online groups attempt to empower individuals they will often do so by featuring the singular rhetorician on their website, giving them a column, and so on, but massive anonymous groups simply give their combined voice to them. This means that no one can ask why we should listen to the empowered voice—in fact, it may be impossible to tell that they have not been part of the group all along.

For example, Anonymous has turned its collective eye toward specific animal abusers several times in the past decade. When a video was released online that showed a young girl throwing puppies into a river and laughing about it, members helped on several different forums to find her identity and attempt to get her charged with animal abuse in her country (Chen, 2010). They were ultimately successful.

Every once in a while, though, that video reemerges and goes viral again with new users that do not realize that it was already taken care of. When this happens it causes new rage across new groups—most recently on Facebook groups amongst dog-lovers. These groups that are not anonymous (as Facebook tends not to be) and do not have the power of a large group identity or, indeed, many thousands of members, stereotypically will talk about what *should* be done to someone who takes joy in throwing puppies in a river but do not actually do anything to find out who the girl is or even to discover that she has been prosecuted already. They fail at looking up the video at Snopes to see if it is a hoax, or even that it is now five years old. Groups that use real identities might have more accountability, but they are also harder to move to action (and are less likely to take action). The bystander effect may be greater within groups of named individuals than within anonymous groups. Groups with greater personal accountability (and less group identity and power) are good at discussing issues but are less likely to actually do something with that discussion.

Taking the name "Anonymous" or any other name that is meaningless to us lends us rhetorical strength in that it separates us from our claim. Online rhetoric relies less upon ethos and more upon numbers, entertainment value, and novelty. By taking on an anonymous name, we gain numbers and power while being united under a single voice. By using memes, we gain entertainment value. By allowing mass scale unmoderated content to survive, we gain novelty and allow for creativity. When these needs are met, large numbers of people can be convinced to, say, create a cat macro, protest the Church of Scientology, or find a young man and lend him some porn.

If writing teachers have a goal of working with students who are being taught to take political action when appropriate, they may wish to look at anonymity and large groups as one way to encourage that action. Bystander syndrome can be used in our favor as well as against us—while members of large anonymous groups in person are less likely to take action if no one else does, members of large anonymous groups online are *more likely* to take action if they see other people doing so. Working with large groups also allows us to reduce the cost to our own individual identities as well.

In *What Video Games Have to Teach Us About Learning and Literacy*, James Paul Gee (2003) writes about the multiple identities that gamers take on. In our metaphor of Internet as game, we can also extend these identities into Internet spaces for the sake of thinking about this phenomenon further. When playing roleplaying games, Gee recognizes three identities: one is the gamer as they are in the real world, one is the avatar on the screen, and the third is the projected identity of gamer *into* the avatar. At the same time, Phillips (2015) writes of the "trolling mask," the projected identity of the gamer into the avatar. The avatar is the mask they wear to be able to troll without it affecting their real-world identity. Phillips is repeatedly amazed at how trolls separate their trolling identity from themselves. They will speak about one of the pseudonyms they take on as if that person is a completely different person, giving the credit for their victories and lulz to their favorite personal pseudonymous Facebook account, for example. This is their avatar identity. This identity play may be a key to the emotional detachment that trolls have with their online actions.

In some large online ad-hoc groups, a single identity is held by many thousands of people. A person might project their identity into that group—or not. Some people see themselves as fully participating members of the group (and probably attend meet-ups or go to real world events and protests if possible), seeing Anonymous as a part of them in the way that Gee imagines that his avatar Bead-bead is a part of him and vice-versa. However, still others can probably play with the identity that Anonymous wants them to take on without ever really considering themselves as being projected into it (or even a part of it). For some group members, identity and engagement (and immersion) in the group is simply more important than to others.

So are They Good or Bad?

There has been a decent amount of coverage of Anonymous in popular media in the past few years, suggesting that their vigilantism has garnered attention that their original roots in attacking private individuals never would have. However, even if we can deem the sort of organization they have and the sort of game they play as neutral or even good for procedural rhetoric, can we judge this group and others like it?

4Chan and the newer 9GAG still participate in a lot of trolling—messing with peoples' lives for the hell of it. They have been behind several hoaxes and raids that were unpolitically motivated unlike a lot of Anonymous's recent work. They also have been heavily involved in GamerGate.

Social media is especially easy to commandeer for almost any purpose—real or not. In publicizing rape cases, Anonymous used the exact methods that 4Chan had before (an IRC Channel devoted to talking about the case and various social media) to force media attention upon the issue. The *same* procedures have been used in other countries—particularly those with controlling governments that do not allow for freedom of information access online—to distribute news stories and stand up against totalitarian governments. In China, proxy servers are used to access Twitter, Facebook, and other services that allow dissidents to communicate (Parker, 2014). In a book published in 2014, Emily Parker interviews dissidents from China, Cuba, and other totalitarian countries that use the Internet to communicate and organize. Dissidents have been given a way, through this technology, to know "who their comrades are" (Parker, 2014, loc 222).

To understand these procedures—in that they can be used for good or bad—I would like to examine them outside of value judgment. In chapters 4 and 5, I would like to examine some specific procedures in use in these and other raids (and examples from other sources as well) to discuss how they function. In so doing, we can look at how these procedures can be rhetorical and algorithmic while recognizing that the game they metaphorically belong to is neither in total good or bad—but deserves study despite its wide variety of applications.

4 Rules and Procedures of the Internet

Analyzing the rules by which a game is created is a key component to analyzing a system procedurally. So, let us first take a deeper look at the list of the Rules of the Internet (while the trolling lexicon is much larger, this is a good place to start), before looking at specific procedures. While humorous and not meant to all be taken at face value, the Rules of the Internet are really the only written document that states the purpose and governing ideas of this specific ad-hocracy. Other rules are also unwritten and represented purely by the actions the group has taken—bullies will not be tolerated, free speech is the only option for Internet systems, animal abuse is not tolerated, etc.

First, let us ask what the rules of the system are. The rules of the system recreate only selectively some parts of the world and not others (Gee, 2003). The Internet as a game, then, is going to not only recreate some parts of the world but also some parts of the Internet—other parts would not be acceptable as part of the game, coherent within it, seen as viable, or even needed. They are not the procedures that people follow to play (join this group, post this meme here, make memes when possible), but lay out the conditions by which a group wins or loses, what they believe, what play looks like, and so on. They create the world that the game is in.

So, when the first rules are dedicated to defining what not to talk about, that anonymity is important, this is a key part of the identity of anyone playing the game. By taking on the name "Anonymous," each member of the ad-hoc does three things: (1) Becomes more powerful than they would be on their own as many people can post under this singular name, (2) becomes not only a part of the ad-hoc, but a part of the singular identity that speaks with one voice that is Anonymous online (without tracking IP addresses it would be difficult to tell when multiple people are posting under the same name), and (3) forgoes their past identity. When members accept the rules they become part of the whole—at least theoretically. When Phillips (2015) notes that many trolls talk about their trolling identities as completely other people, that is because in many ways they are—they are as much an avatar as Mario, Yoshi, or a Sackboy.

The first rules ("do not talk about /b/") also immediately make a pop-culture reference (to *Fight Club*) and therefore also set up that other such references, to other pop culture, would probably be valued. It might even be impossible to "play" from a non-anonymous name or pseudonym.

Anonymous itself is not gendered or raced—Guy Fawkes masks aside. Some media members assume these are young white men, nearly always "living in their mother's basement," but that is not only unproven but has been actively disproven when women and people of color appear at Anonymous rallies. However, at the same time that they are neither gendered nor raced, they are sometimes both misogynistic and racist. Without a leader or figurehead, the mob can and has turned in many different directions. This is backed up by Rule 6: "Anonymous can be a horrible, senseless, uncaring monster" (2013). There is no way to protect yourself, truly, from becoming a target of Anonymous other than simply not talking about anything online at all—and what fun is that? Phillips (2015) notes that most of the people she has interviewed about 4Chan are men, though there are a few women in her study as well. I feel like it is almost necessary to point out that there are female Anons, especially after the media has (recently) cast nearly all of 4Chan in the same light as its board r9k—which is all about being a white male outcast. While those things might describe most of the people on some boards, there are others that are more gender neutral. Additionally, Anonymous as an ethical body has attracted numerous women as they slowly have started taking on more humanitarian and sometimes feminist goals.

Many of the rules have come about because of common anti-rhetorical fallacies employed by people online—they are effective and have been written down as "rules" because of their success but also as a reminder to not take such attacks personally. These rules, when used procedurally, create a system where rhetorical moves are systematized and large groups of people can easily argue with one voice. This voice is not complicated though—complicated rhetorical moves would be difficult if not impossible for a group with no official leadership to organize. Furthermore, if people want to go outside of the rules for whatever reason when posting, the Rules of the Internet allow for that: "There are no real rules about posting" (Rule 8, Rules of the Internet, 2013).

Let's examine these "rhetorical" procedures more closely. Rules 11–21 (or so) deal explicitly with posting and arguments:

1. All your carefully picked arguments can easily be ignored.

2. Anything you say can and will be used against you.

3. Anything you say can be turned into something else—fixed.

4. Do not argue with trolls—it means they win.

5. The harder you try the harder you will fail.

6. If you fail in epic proportions, it may just become a winning failure.

7. Every win fails eventually.

8. Everything that can be labeled can be hated.

9. The more you hate it the stronger it gets.

10. Nothing is to be taken seriously.

11. Original content is original only for a few seconds before getting old. (Rules of the Internet, 2013)

In analyzing a game rhetorically, Bogost (2007) instructs us to not only consider who has made the game or the culture from which the game has emerged (engaging with *ethos* or the rhetorical triangle), but also to look carefully at what claims about the world the rules of the system create. We also should consider why these rules were chosen over others.

So what type of argumentative game do the Rules of the Internet create? First, if your arguments are to be driven by traditional rhetorics they will not be convincing to any part of your audience that enjoys trolling. Even if they are, trolls will be able to ignore them. Trolls are unlikely to pick on weak arguments for fun—people without a strong sense of rhetoric or with a weak argumentative voice won't be fun for trolls for long. In some ways this means that the presence of trolls at a site for a long period of time probably means that the original rhetor is being persuasive to some part of the audience—but the masses of trolls aren't part of it. This creates a "world" where the best arguments made by otherwise good rhetoricians are torn apart and reviled. "Players" of the game may end up feeling like everything they say opens them to attack. In the case of feminist women this often leaves them feeling like they can't talk at all—once targeted, even otherwise harmless statements can be used against the rhetor.

The Game of the Internet is chaotic—easy editing of posts and anonymous or throwaway accounts mean that many people can come to a site very quickly and tear apart rigidly organized structure in little to no time. Ad-Hocs that are strong one day might be weak the next as they break apart and reform somewhere else. Some players will get involved in any argument—not caring who is hurt in the process. For them it is as simple as switching out a disc or cartridge in a game—one day they are "killing" Nazis and the next attacking brightly colored evil unicorns, the target doesn't matter as much as the game does to them. Furthermore, even in the middle of a raid, the rules can change rapidly. Unlike traditional rhetorical systems (with somewhat rigid rhetorical structures), trolling and gaming rhetorics are controlled by the trolls. Trolls can change the rules at any time to force a win in their favor (Phillips, 2015). They simply aren't playing by the same rules as everyone else.

By taking yourself seriously (by making serious arguments on your website) you open yourself to attack by *standing for something*. It didn't take trolls long to learn that people will defend their tightly held viewpoints far more strongly than those that they don't really care about. They know they can upset the real live people behind the website in question by attacking those viewpoints the people care about the most. This doesn't vary whether they are attacking radical feminists for their radical feminism or rape apologists for standing up for rapists and bullies—whatever you believe in most is your greatest weakness.

In some ways, arguing online is like being trained to play one game and then trying to play by the rules of that game in a completely different environment. Imagine if you had only ever played Mario games or other side scrolling platform games. To kill enemies you jump on their heads. Sometimes you get special power-ups. However, in the absence of those power-ups you are left with one weapon—your feet. You don't even have a gun. Having played as Mario for your entire life (perhaps even earning a doctorate in Yoshi-Studies), you are suddenly dropped into *Gears of War* (a first-person shooter). You see an enemy and run at them. You are shot and die. You try again—with much the same result. You duck behind some crates. What now? You jump and stomp on the crates and reveal a gun. Great! However, you find the gun is entirely the wrong size for your body, and you cannot fire it very well with your round hands (Mario has very oddly-shaped hands). You look around and can't find a fire flower. You literally cannot play in this environment because you have not been taught how, do not know the rules, and the rules you have been taught to abide by are actually harmful. Instead of doing damage to enemies you are doing nothing but damaging yourself.

Using traditional rhetoric online works much the same way. Relying upon logic, emotion, and even your own real-world reputation is unlikely to work in a world with completely different rules.

According to Bogost, video games do not recreate the world, they choose which elements of the world to very selectively model (2007). So "[p]rocedural representation models only some subset of a source system, in order to draw attention to that portion as the subject of the representation" (2007, p. 46). Trolls might be arguing for "lulz," but they are also drawing attention to a weakness in our current rhetorical model—it cannot stand up to an ad-hoc or to rhetoric that does not care about truth. Procedural rhetorics advance "a claim about how part of the system it represents does, should, or could function" (2007, p. 36). So, part of the claim being made by this type of game is that our current rhetoric as taught and understood in Western society has a weakness in its ability to adapt to numbers, a weakness in its ability to be used by an ad-hoc, and also weaknesses in its ability to adapt to digital systems and pictorial rhetorics like those often used by ad-hocs. When whittled down to the very short (not too long so that everyone will read) and the image (because who reads an article when you can look at a picture?), many of our "strongest" arguments are untranslatable. Into this void has grown a procedural rhetoric fueled by rapidly developing and transforming ad-hocracies.

MEMES TO GAMES

Taking memes created in ad-hocs as an example, let's trace how memes embody procedural rhetoric as well as build a procedural rhetoric for online ad-hocracies. Remember that Ian Bogost first begins to define *procedural rhetoric* using the work of Kenneth Burke:

> He [Burke] extends rhetoric beyond persuasion, instead suggesting "identification" as a key term for the practice. We use symbolic systems, such as language, as a way to achieve this identification. Burke defines rhetoric as a part of the practice of identification, as "the use of words by human agents to form attitudes or induce actions in other human agents." (2007, p. 20)

Both Burke and Bogost see the rhetorical as that which facilitates human action and interaction. In the case of games, Bogost believes that persuasion is less important than the Burkean notion of identification. Rhetoric isn't simply a means to an end, it is "a means to facilitate identification and to 'bridge the conditions of estrangement that are natural and inevitable'" (2007, p. 21). All rhetoric—Burkean and otherwise—requires a skill, a technique—to connect with rhetorical practice. Thus, if games are to have rhetoric there will also be games that use it well and those that do not. However, at this time, it almost seems as though games are seen as lesser forms of expression, something Bogost connects to the fact that most forms of nonverbal expression are seen as inferior to verbal discourse.

Bogost puts the procedure "back" into rhetorical practice. He believes that it is possible to follow rules and use processes persuasively. "Procedural rhetoric is the general name for the practice of authoring arguments through processes" (2007, pp. 28–29). Thus, even outside of games, any time a specific algorithmic process is followed in rhetorical persuasion, that persuasion is using procedural rhetoric:

> Following the classical model, procedural rhetoric entails persuasion—to change opinion or action. Following the contemporary model, procedural rhetoric entails persuasion—to convey ideas effectively. Procedural rhetoric is a subdomain of procedural authorship; its arguments are made not through the construction of words or images, but through the authorship of rules of behavior, the construction of dynamic models. In computation, those rules are authored in code, through the practice of programming. (p. 29)

Procedural rhetoric gives us a power outside of computer programming though. If we expand the definition to those things that follow rules and procedures but are not code, then we gain the ability to make claims about the way things work. Ideally, the term could be applied outside of video games and be used more generally: "Procedurality refers to a way of creating, explaining, or understanding processes" (2007, pp. 2–3). In this case, we are trying to understand the processes that a troll follows when playing the Game of the Internet.

Memes are another way to proceduralize rhetoric. Instead of using a wiki that tells members of a site how to attack a target and what to say when they do, memes create quick and easy messages. For the purpose of this discussion, image macros will be discussed as the most common Internet meme. At the time of this writing, services available online allow users to upload pictures and add text to them or to choose from already "memetic" images that have been uploaded by other users and given meaning by the community (the most popular is Meme Generator). Because these are so easy to create and post and because they rely upon audience members recognizing them as already memetic (or at least making an attempt at being memetic), they speak to a very specific group of people online—those people who are part of the game of memes or at least find them funny. Image-macro memes can be employed for fun or for serious purposes, but because they are usually associated with fun they are not usually derided for being "too serious" or even attacked by trolls in the way a blog post might be.

One of the interesting abilities that 4Chan and other ad-hocs display is a great proclivity for creation. In addition to taking part in creating the Rules of the Internet, as was noted in past chapters, they have also been involved in creating most of the popular Internet memes in the past decade. The creative energy sparked by the Game of the Internet should not be ignored. Within its gamespace, because there is no moderation and supposedly free speech reigns (within a certain set of mostly non-serious, non-sensical guidelines, of course), a number of interesting genres have appeared that were created by the users for the users from the game.

Lolcat images are one such instance. These are now just one of many types of images composed in a similar manner—although the originals were just cats plus text. Rules govern the creation of memes, which have been built into the online engines that can now be used to create them. However, those rules grew organically from the discussion of the ad-hoc about the images they found funny, reposted, and even upvoted on other sites. Those rules were unwritten until formalized in the sites that can create them without image-editing software but are no less easy to understand than more formal rules of play for the Internet. Clay Shirky, in writing about Lolcats, notes that

> Lolcat images, dumb as they are, have internal rules, everything from "Captions should be spelled phonetically" to "The lettering should use a sans-serif font." Even at the stipulated depths of stupidity, in other words, there are ways to do a locat wrong, which means there are ways to do it right, which means there is some metric of quality, even if limited. (2010, p. 20)

Shirky notes that text placed on the photos should be a certain type of font (this has been narrowed even further by the Cheeseburger Network and other sites that allow you to build an image macro directly on their website). The text should also be white with a black border on a darker picture. Shirky goes on to say "However little the world needs the next lolcat, the message *You can play this game too* is a change from what we're used to in the media landscape. The stupidest possible creative act is still a creative act" (2010, p. 20). In creating genres that inspire ordinary Internet users to be creative themselves, the Game of the Internet allows players to create viral media (or media more likely to go viral). Why does a lolcat go viral (or a bad real-estate listing, or a funny quote from a student paper)? And why are we not studying more deeply why some memes become viral and instead dismissing them as not very useful when creating viral Internet phenomena and communicating arguments very quickly online to a large audience is *very useful* to anyone who wants to be persuasive online? Shirky goes on:

However, making the Lolcat is only half the fun.

> The pleasure in *You can play this game too* isn't just in the mak-
> ing, it's also in the sharing. . . . Lolcats aren't just user-generated,
> they are user-shared. The sharing, in fact, is what makes the
> making fun—no one would create a lolcat to keep for them-
> selves. (Shirky, 2010, p. 19)

If you think of the Internet as a game, then you too must consider the fact that there are other players out there ready to interact with you. In fact, the whole point of playing most games is to share the experience with others. Even if you play *Tetris*, you might very well talk about *Tetris* with another person or strive to beat their score.

Unlike *Tetris*, however, in this game you can create too. While Shirky seems to believe that most people create from the memes that already have rules laid down for them, this is not always the case. Image macros can be very useful for complaining about things, as is easy to see from even a brief perusal of any meme site. People sympathize very easily with others' problems. In fact, similar image macros have started to be used by feminists on feminist websites to educate about privilege (male and white primarily).

The best example is called "Privilege Denying Dude" (PDD). PDD was created by a feminist who was tired of white men in life and online saying privileged statements and claiming that they, themselves, were entirely feminist and anti-racist. She took a stock photo (that was purchased legally), put it on a colored background, and used the standard blocky white font that has become ubiquitous with memes and images macros. On top of this man she posted things like "If we had a white entertainment network that would be racist . . . unfair!" "Your idea sounds so much better when I rephrase it," and "If what I say offends anyone, I'm sorry you're too sensitive" (Know Your Meme, 2011). These images make use of the play available online, of the Game of the Internet, all the while making a political statement against a common type of individual.

The meme became far more popular than the original creator ever intended. Thousands of feminists and anti-racists flocked to the generator available on the author's Tumblr site to put in their own annoyances. The images that resulted could be easily used in anti-racist and feminist teachings—also many of them are just funny.

Indeed, the meme created a public uproar from the individuals that it was meant to mock. Men complained about being mocked, much to the mockers' glee. The conversations that resulted not only proved the meme-creators' point, they made a lot of people look very foolish for espousing one opinion while unwittingly demonstrating another. In short, they got trolled. They proved that the meme was right and necessary in their trying to protest it. (This is not—though sometimes is—the case in trolling against women. Why? Well—it's easy to prove that someone thinks that a white entertainment network is necessary and needs to exist and poke fun at that. It's a lot harder to suggest that someone be raped and then somehow *prove* they deserve that treatment. While rape and murder are tremendously powerful silencing tools, they aren't very good tools when used to expose actual invalid thought processes. This falls apart in extreme conservative trolling, however, where the troll believes that all women who physically fall outside of some fairly rigid guidelines deserve poor treatment.) The creator of PDD still believes, however, that due to the meme's popularity it will be used ultimately to show these individuals that their position is mockable and worth changing—and hopes that their position will someday be changed.

The power of memes and playing by the Rules should not be ignored by any group, but especially those previously marginalized online like women and minorities. PDD became so popular so quickly that the creator's Tumblr had to be deactivated to preserve bandwidth, and she was also asked to stop using the stock photo she purchased. Why? The website that she bought it from felt that it could be damaging to the individual in the picture to be included in such a ubiquitous meme (while it would be just fine, say, if his picture were to be used in a billboard about herpes because it would be seen by far fewer people). He was replaced by a pro-feminist actor, although many of the original images still exist. Today there are also new versions of the meme that feature a white woman who ignores transgender issues and spouts racist statements.

Why do some people like online environments and games while others fail to see the point of them entirely? Perhaps it is simply because some people haven't tried to play with them and in them enough. Sitting down at a computer is not the same thing as becoming immersed in the society that the computer has enabled and the game that the society has created. In the case of memes, it is easy to dismiss them as easy and silly (as Shirky does), but they can actually be used to transmit complex ideas (like privilege) and should be fully considered by all people interested in social justice online as at least a secondary communication medium.

In 2015, many of my students who are interested in social justice learn about racism, feminism, and other forms of discrimination via Tumblr. Their first interaction with these concepts is not coming from classrooms as often as it is from the Internet. We might complain about "Tumblr Feminism" being reductive, reactive, and extreme, but it would be more effective to reach out and start communicating and arguing within these same systems as they emerge. If "Tumblr Feminism" is angry (sometimes to the point of blaming other feminists for not being feminist enough, which is certainly a thing I face when I work with young women today), ignoring the medium is unlikely to bring those women learning about feminism closer to the rest of the group in a procedural way. The procedures followed often seem to be along the lines of "unequivocally hate and stand against these things" where "these things" are things like "man-spreading" (a term I'm still sure will vanish into the ether soon enough) and "man-splaining." While these are real enough problems, they might pale in comparison to working on equal pay at a university or prison reform. However, many online feminisms of the current moment rely upon procedural reactions (when you see X do Y and feel Z) to be effective, and should not be ignored for it. Much like the other ad-hocs seen here, these are powerful movements because of their numbers and because so many people can identify with them.

Although *ad hominem* and *ad baculum* are generally seen as fallacious and therefore not rhetorical, these fallacies can function procedurally. In this chapter I will discuss some of the most common methods by which individuals, groups, and websites are threatened and harassed and examine how these procedures are meant to work as well as some ways they might be retaliated against.

All of these procedures can be considered as game-like, even though some might have real-world legal and moral consequences. However, if the Internet is a game—or is seen through a lens of gaming—then these are just some of the potential offensive attacks that might be available to a player.

Banhammer/Silencing

Although most of the groups that I study allow for anonymous posting (by necessity) or allow users to choose a different pseudonym every time they visit, sites that are pseudonymous are probably some of the most popular online, second at this time only to social networking sites that encourage the use of real-world identities. To keep people from constantly creating new accounts, many sites that have users create a username encourage them to keep that singular username for an extended period of time by attaching points, "karma," or other digital rewards for posting quality content that other users like. Although "throwaway" accounts can be created by users for controversial topics, overwhelmingly they are encouraged to use their main username for the sites to amass these points in their own primary name as often as possible.

People become attached to these identities, and in some places whatever points that are earned can even get users access to special forums and abilities. On Reddit, users that really like a post can buy the person who made it "Reddit Gold," which gives them special access to a forum for other gold posters for one month and helps fund the site. In other places, users' ratings are visible on every post they make, which means that other people might listen to them more or less based upon how their written content has already been judged by others.

One of the primary procedures used to silence dissenters on web forums is to simply "ban" them. Users who have been banned are unable to post and unable to speak. They lose their voice entirely. In some places they also will have their IP address banned, so if they would like to post again they have to either use a proxy, create an account at a school or another location that has a different IP address, or wait until they are no longer banned. Most forums include a set of rules with information both about how to behave and how to avoid being banned.

On some sites those rules seem to be completely arbitrary. Each sub-section of Reddit (referred to as a sub-reddit or "sub" for short) can set its own rules and appoint moderators who enforce those rules. For example, I have been banned from a Pomeranian forum for suggesting that I did not want to see people's dead dogs. It turns out they thought I was referencing a man who posted pictures of his animal as she was about to die—I was actually referring to someone who posted a picture of their animal on its funeral pyre in their backyard. Regardless, I was not allowed back in.

Moderators (or "mods") are nearly always seen as the enemy, the enforcers, and those who are out to ruin other people's fun. Moderation, as such, is very lax in some places purely because Internet users seem to currently believe that moderation ruins communities by banning voices instead of supporting communities by making interesting conversation. Free speech is valued over community in many places online.

So, unlike the other communities already talked about here, the Banhammer requires moderation, rules, and accounts. Applying the "Banhammer" is the act of banning temporarily or permanently any users who do not follow rules and procedures that are present on the site, or do not subscribe to the dominant ideology of the site. A true ad-hocracy cannot develop if a moderation team is in place that does not allow it to. If conversation goes to a place the moderation team wants to prevent, it becomes easy for them to simply silence everyone that disagrees with them. While this keeps a "nicer" and more polite community, it does not usually allow for the massive amounts of play and creativity that occur on other (unmoderated) forums.

Despite this, banning is used procedurally in two ways:

1. Although the Rules of the Internet state that Anonymous is not your personal army, banning and strict moderation can create "hive minds" driven by single ideologies. While Anonymous is fairly amorphous and has taken on many different political stances over the years of its existence, moderated communities generally will be ideology-driven, and if the users' belief in that ideology wanes the community will break apart and vanish as well. However, such communities can be even more vicious in their attacks upon those that disagree with them—they can control their own space, but they wish to control the spaces of others as well.

2. Users will enter a space that is not ideologically consistent with their own and attempt to *be banned*. Becoming banned can be, at time, a procedural technique of its own. Being banned is a response, after all, from the site under attack. Therefore, one procedure related to the Banhammer is to go to a site, set up an account, and say things to anger and hurt people until banned, then do it again. This procedure is best used *en masse* and can significantly wear upon moderation staff and can eventually silence other members of the community when moderation eventually fails.

The Banhammer is procedural because it follows the tightly written rules of the community. If moderators talk to people before banning them, or attempt to teach them the rules of the community, that is *not* a Banhammer. The Banhammer refers to a procedural rhetorical move in which the offending party is instantly silenced for making an offensive gesture or statement.

Because this type of moderation is so strict, it can often be done by a computer. Auto-moderation is available for some communities. On the AskWomen subreddit, any mention of "bitching" or other "gendered slurs" will automatically get the comment removed and hidden from other users. This is done by a computer—not by a person—in hopes of keeping moderation staff un-fatigued. The silencing is instantaneous, and people must ask for permission to repost their material after whatever offensive term has been removed from it. Although, saying that someone else called you a slut is considered okay by the rules, the auto-moderator will often delete those posts as well.

The Banhammer is generally recognized as one way to deal with trolls in online spaces. After all, if they cannot make comments anymore, they won't be a problem. However, in reality their game is set up in such a way that being banned is like winning—sure they have to create a new account, but they know that they got to you. They will make another account (or four) and invite many of their friends to do the same. The Banhammer, therefore, should not be deployed against trolls unless you want your computer system or mods to have to do a lot more banning in the near future.

DOXXING

Doxxing (dox = documents) is a popular procedural trope wherein one party will post the personal details of the other online—generally contact information and/or financial information, but also sometimes the names and contact information of parents, employers, etc. Other trolls are invited to call, harass, and generally attempt to ruin the life of the person who has been doxxed. Financial accounts may be hacked, threats are called directly to a house, and this is likely combined with other types of harassment such as sending lots of free boxes for mail pick up or ordering many pizzas in the name of the person doxxed.

One of the most famous incidents of doxxing happened to Kathy Sierra—a once popular Internet feminist and blogger. She was doxxed by "weev," a black-hat hacker and anon. In 2008, the *New York Times* wrote that weev was taking credit for having posted Kathy Sierra's address and Social Security Number online, along with a fake account of her career accusing her of being a sex worker (Schwartz, 2008). He also may have written false claims of abuse towards her daughters (Dean, 2010).

Before the attacks, Sierra was running a technology blog called *Creating Passionate Users*; however, some people online did not think that she was technologically savvy enough to be garnering the praise and speaking engagements that she got. She was threatened with death and a picture of her with a noose around her neck was posted (see the section on death and rape threats above). She was terrified and cancelled several speaking engagements. Unsurprisingly, harassment increased after this was reported about in the news, and she was quoted as saying that she felt unsafe to leave her house or yard. She deleted the blog and left the Web (BBC, 2007). This was followed by her being doxxed.

Another famous case of doxxing occurred during GamerGate. GamerGate is a movement that concerns itself with video game journalism ethics. As someone who has both actively tried to get review copies of games for the academic journal *Kairos*—I know that big game companies are not remotely interested in giving away free copies to academics who, for one, might publish neutral or negative reviews or, for two, won't publish for months if not years. Games sites are faced by some of the same issue even if their publication schedule is quicker. GamerGate has roots in harassment that Zoe Quinn, a female game developer (independent) who created a game on Twine called *Depression Quest* (2013), went through as a result of releasing that game (and breaking up with her boyfriend). Twine is an easy-to-use game engine that can make simple decision-based text games. It can also build games with videos, objects, and even simple GUIs—but most people use it to build text-based games. *Depression Quest* (2013) was created with the support of David Lindsey (writing) and Isaac Shankler (music), and it got popular because despite being available free to play online, Quinn and her team got it accepted on the Steam store.

Being featured there gave the game validity that most Twine games don't have. Realistically, creating a game on Twine does not require coding and generally is not very difficult, so it is unsurprising that there was some backlash about such a game being featured in a popular online game shop and interface. However, it was featured because some people felt that it helped them work through issues they were having with depression and also helped other people understand what loved ones were going through. Hardcore gamers, however, regard text-based games as a relic of the 1970s and 1980s, not something to be paid for on Steam. She began to receive death threats and harassment. Around this same time, Eron Gjoni, her ex-boyfriend, wrote a long series of blog entries about her that accused her of cheating—especially of sleeping with someone to get a positive game review for *Depression Quest* (Hathaway, 2014). Although it was later discovered that the man who she was accused of sleeping with never wrote a review of her game, the damage was done.

In GamerGate, you can see the results of death and rape threats, the Banhammer (naturally early threats were deleted and posters banned), and also doxxing. She was nearly immediately doxxed, with her address and phone number posted. Her relatives were called and told she was a slut. She left her home and has been couch surfing in an attempt to stop the harassment. Later, Anita Sarkeesian was similarly doxxed and driven from her home. Another games' journalist that referred to gaming being "dead" became a target (Alexander, 2014). Later still, women who starred in popular sci-fi film remakes and reboots such as *Ghostbusters* and *Star Wars* became victims of similar harassment and attacks for "ruining" these films. While academics are fully familiar with the act of referring to dead media alongside the dead author (Barthes, 1967), gamers who were already incensed about what they saw as feminist domination of their spaces took to the internet to fight for their games that glorified money, women, guns, and violence (Alexander, 2014).

Doxxing is destructive—though it has also been leveled for good. During the protests in Ferguson, Missouri, police officers with ties to the KKK were doxxed. In this case, the documents shared were not just their contact information but the proof of their connection to the Klan. Doxxing is being used increasingly by liberal organizations as a method of public dissent, and unless it is made specifically illegal is likely one we will see grow in the future. Similarly, the long list of media men who have been accused of sexual harassment and violence has also been made public—but not all of the crimes listed on that document are sexual in nature, nor are all of them actionable. As such, this doxxing may yet prove to be less positive than it was initially seen as by feminists.

THREATS OF BODILY HARM AS RHETORICAL TROPE

Since the very early days of anonymous networked dialogue, one way to silence, shock, and hurt people has been to threaten to rape them. Julian Dibbell wrote about that "first" rape wherein an avatar was overtaken and raped in LamdaMOO (1999). Today it is the single term most used against women online—if you are female and hold an opinion openly online someone has probably threatened to rape you, while both women and men are likely to receive death threats or other threats of bodily harm. In the over two hundred pages of deleted emails and comments that I received from BB, rape (often misspelled "raep") was the most common threat that she received. During GamerGate, Zoe Quinn published the planning conversation on IRC (more about this later)—and rape is mentioned in some form 607 times. Phillips (2015) notes that rape is threatened because it is the *worst thing possible to say*—with many men still believing that to be raped is worse than being killed, it should not be surprising that threatening rape is a common trope in online trolling.

This is, of course, awful—and I would never suggest that it is not. Rape is life destroying, underreported, and obviously a point of contention online. Mention a woman being raped online and people will be quick to remind you that men are raped too, and often note that *more* men are raped if you count prison statistics (sources both for and against this claim are numerous). However, I don't think that should stop us from viewing why this single threat is the most popularly used rhetorical one—why does threatening rape or other bodily harm have the power that it does? Why is threatening rape the surest way to shut down and silence women, and what can we do to stop it?

First, in my procedurally rhetorical systems, threatening rape is par for the course. In any argument with a woman (or when playing a video game with women even), threatening rape will often get the woman to leave. This is simply one word that many women will not stand for—leaving raids when other members of the raid begin talking about how they will rape the opponent (defeat them) is not terribly unusual. The term carries an unusual amount of weight and power and so therefore is one of those that is used in online arguments often—it is easy to say, the man (or sometimes woman) saying it does so generally with the understanding that they won't actually rape the person they are saying it to. Some trolls are even willing to fake rapeto gain sympathy and power, and it is little wonder that they might assume that others do the same.

Many of those that say it don't really understand why it bears the rhetorical weight that it does—they just know it is effective (these are, of course, assumptions—but these are safe assumptions to make considering that I have personally had children under the age of thirteen threaten to rape me while playing online games, and they clearly did not have any perception of the weight of their threat. They only knew that saying it would make most women upset or angry and wished to make me upset and angry.)

In terms of fighting real rape, whether or not Anonymous's campaigns in cities like Maryville and Steubenville will be ultimately effective remains to be seen. In terms of fighting "rape culture" (the phrase used to describe the set of cultural practices that blames the victim of rape and knowingly or unknowingly supports, normalizes, and tolerates rape), the use of the word so easily to shut down conversation with women is still problematic. Because of this, telling a woman to ignore these threats and "not feed the trolls" when it is used is, perhaps, not the best advice to give because ignoring them or leaving the conversation just adds to the power of using rape threats to shut down conversation online. Phillips (2015) argues that the media empowers us to joke about rape when it gives voice to people like Todd Aiken—a congressman who noted that the female body naturally had a way of "shutting down" a pregnancy that was caused by rape (p. 158). She believes that as long as the media gives a voice to people like him and other conservative media mouthpieces, we will also have trolls "fighting back" with rape threats. So long as the media will get up in arms about rape threats, the logic goes, then rape threats will be made. " . . . so long as mainstream institutions are steered by people who behave like trolls, there will always be an audience of trolls primed to maximize mainstream ugliness" (Phillips, 2015, p. 158). So though I would like to echo such an easily executable advisory as "ignore it," with the hope of giving less of a voice to the ugliness, I'm not sure it is so simple.

If any term needs to be systematically depowered online it is *rape*. Only in depowering this term will rape culture stop being fed by its use online, and only then will women be able to exist without constantly having rape threatened. However, it cannot easily be reclaimed in the same ways that others have. Women will not chant this term as they do *bitch* or even *cunt* (as they are asked to do in some versions of *The Vagina Monologues*); we cannot reclaim this term—it is not racially derogatory, it is not sexually discriminatory (it *does* happen to men too), it is not even about our genitals, not really (Ensler, 2001). When rape is used as a joke it is still offensive, and women in Western society increasingly do not accept rape jokes. In other words, because rape is an act, reclaiming it (as we have *bitch* somewhat successfully and *slut* less so) is all but impossible. African Americans can reclaim the "n-word," but cannot reclaim any of the many acts of violence perpetrated on themselves or their ancestors. Acts remain powerful when words do not. The words associated with those acts are far more powerful than any word that accusers can label us with.

We need a method by which to reclaim acts without perpetrating those acts on someone else. We need to be able to reclaim rape without committing rape, which would devalue the term.

Discussing rape culture has made the term more popular, and indeed, that is important work. However, it has not made the term undismissible by opponents of feminist work. It is very easy to claim that "rape culture" is a term made up by feminists to entrap men, or to claim that all men are rapists. The specter of Dworkin (2007) is still invoked by people online who have probably never read her work and believe that the sole argument she made is that all sex is rape. Others seem to believe that *all* feminists hate men and think that all sex is rape.

At the same exact time, some people who might have been drawn to this style of trolling (and no doubt some who are) are joining causes against actual rapists. Yet, these same groups contain many individuals who would not be upset by a man who threatens to rape a woman online. They are more upset (often to a great deal of action) if they hear that porn is taken away from a young boy or man than they are if a woman receives a rape threat. They understand rape procedurally online as being different from rape in real life—for them there is a disconnect between the word and the act, or the word online and the act in real life.

Should women similarly separate the act and the procedure? I'm not so sure. As I mentioned above, some sort of reclaiming/depowering of the term online would be the best action to take. Currently, women are given a lot of advice about how to deal with such threats. In an article called "Why Women Aren't Welcome on the Internet," Amanda Hess suggests that women are typically told to either ignore threats or do anything and everything possible to land all harassers and online stalkers in jail (2014). She specifically states that some of her friends believe such threats are just a "silly game," and that they are best ignored.

But what if it really is not a silly game? What if, instead, it is a *real game*, using rhetorics in the ways that games do, that are truly persuasive, and truly silence people? What then should be the response? Should those same rhetorics be used in rejoinder? Hess reports on Danielle Citron's work, who suggests in a 2009 paper in the *Michigan Law Review* that online abuse, including rape and death threats, can be legally considered discrimination against women's employment opportunities in the same way that Title VII of the Civil Rights Act of 1964 has been used to stop Ku Klux Klan members from protesting around and threatening the workplaces of people of color (2014). How? These threats stop women from being able to work and write online freely because of their gender. At the very least, Hess states that women cannot be at ease online and that further legal action must become possible. It also is possible that if the woman (or man) being silenced through threats of rape is a university student that she or he could file for a Title IX investigation if the threats interrupt his or her schooling.

But laws cannot entirely control behavior, and furthermore I would argue that rape is still different than many of the other *ad hominem* and even the other *ad baculum* attacks. Rape is best compared to death threats and other threats of bodily harm online, though it carries separate cultural capital. Public and private threats of bodily harm create real fear—as people never know when online threats may be carried out in real life. While Julian Dibbell felt physically affronted by the rape of an online character, people online today fear that someone will read public online threats and decide to carry them out, or take online procedures for attacks and bring them into the real world.

People's inability to defend against this threat adequately could, in fact, lead to some women and men re-empowering themselves through false rape reporting. Though rare (2–8%), such reports do exist and have been the subject of a lot of media coverage in the past decade (Lonsway,

Archambault, & Lisak, 2009). Rape takes power away from the victim, while reporting a rape ostensibly takes power away from the perpetrator. Though false rape accusations would seem to empower the disenfranchised, in the real world they cast doubt upon all victims and therefore actually take away even more of the rhetorical strength from people who need it the most. Additionally, threatening a false rape accusation online to an anonymous mob would ultimately do nothing to that mob. In short, though it is possible that some people have taken to using these threats to punish or regain power, they are not effective and should not be seen as rhetorical recourse, procedural or otherwise.

DOC DUMPING

Because Zoe Quinn was familiar with the way 4Chan worked prior to the start of GamerGate, she was able to collect evidence of what was being done to her as far as planning harassment, doxxing, and raids that were being organized by her ex-boyfriend. Initially she posted screenshots of IRC channels where they were planning, and of course said screenshots were logically and rhetorically cherry-picked to prove her point. However, the trolls made a mistake and posted the entire chat log, claiming that it proved that they were right and she was falsifying information. The trolls did not believe that anyone would actually read the document.

The full document prints to over 3500 pages. Like 4Chan itself, the conversation is convoluted, full of memes, and hard to follow. The posting of this type of document as a rhetorical trope has become known as *doc dumping*. When GamerGaters asked for proof that her boyfriend was really behind organizing them (do not use Anonymous as your personal army), she did so—but the document is so dense it would be difficult to glean information from it.

This particularly procedural move is actually popular amongst lawyers, where giving the offense all of the information they need but not time to pour through it is a good way to agree to be helpful but not actually provide help (and also not get accused of perjury or obstructing justice). It is also popular today in politics and can be used to affect the world stage—Wikileaks specializes in doc dumping.

In the case of GamerGate, the people who posted the document clearly didn't expect it to be read—but it was. For example, David Futrelle, a writer at *We Hunted the Mammoth*, notes that despite claims that GamerGate is about journalism ethics and corruption, the document is nearly entirely about Quinn and barely at all about the reporter she allegedly seduced (Futrelle, 2014). He uses the numerous times her name comes up as proof of this (which seems somewhat shaky, but can still be seen as significant):

> The name "Zoe" appears 4778 times in the document, more than once per page; by contrast, "Nathan"—the first name of the allegedly corrupt game journalist she allegedly slept with—appears only 108 times. The words "ethics" and "ethical" appear, collectively, only 146 times. (Futrelle, 2014)

He also notes that pictures of her from when she was thirteen were posted, along with more recent nudes. People in the channel also discuss how much fun it will be to ruin her career and how much they hope she kills herself. They also planned out doing things like sending her nudes to people defending her, and some even openly note that they don't care about video games they just want to see her punished.

One of the quotes that Futrelle pulls out shows that the people discussing this in the channel understand their audience well, and they know that they cannot make this all about one woman or else they will not be taken seriously:

> Aug 21 17.23.31 <sarahv> The problem is that making it about Zoe sleeping around amounts to a personal attack which, while funny and something she totally deserves, will hurt our chances of pushing the other point . . .

> Aug 21 17.23.38 <rd0951>./v should be focused on the implications of gaming journalism . . .

> Aug 21 17.23.47 Because SJWs will cherry-pick the /b/ shit posting and say "See? It's sexist MRAs!" (ZoeQuinnText.txt, 2013, as qtd. in Futrelle, 2014)

They also planned for potential future raids:

> Aug 22 04.53.14 Eugh, why would you want to have her on your HDD? . . .

> Aug 22 04.53.45 <The_Remover> because, a couple of months from now, when all this shit has died down, a raid may just be in order . . .

> Aug 22 04.54.10 and i bet her dad doesn't know she did porn . . . (ZoeQuinnText.txt, 2013, as qtd. in Futrelle, 2014).

And they openly discuss trying to get her to kill herself:

> Aug 25 07.18.18 <Logan> Any chance we can get Zoe to commit suicide?

> Aug 25 07.18.29 if we can get more daming evidence

> Aug 25 07.18.29 I think the [doxxing info removed by DF] is a good shot.

> Aug 25 07.18.33 <temet> like her fucking a train of lack dudes . . .

> Aug 25 07.18.39 <PaperDinosaur> fuck off Logan

> Aug 25 07.18.39 <temet> black

> Aug 25 07.18.51 <Logan> Nah 21st century doing a train is so 90s. . . .

> Aug 25 07.18.59 <PaperDinosaur> If she commits suicide we lose everything . . .

> Aug 25 07.20.34 <PaperDinosaur> If you can't see how driving Zoe to suicide would fuck this entire thing up then you're a fucking idiot

> Aug 25 07.20.41 Imagine the kotaku article . . .

> Aug 25 07.20.48 <temet> PaperDinosaur is right

> Aug 25 07.20.51 <temet> not the right PR play (ZoeQuinnText. txt, 2013, as qtd. in Futrelle, 2014)

Really, the document provided all the evidence that GamerGate was not what it seemed (even though, as I noted earlier, there is corruption in reviews of media in general that *could* be dealt with by an ad-hoc—just not this one). However, the document being published didn't kill Gamer-Gate, nor did it convince anyone who did not want to be convinced.

People in the chat even go ahead and conjecture that Quinn made up the page herself, and that Eron does not exist, "Aug 24 02.58.14 <Cameralady> what if eron is entirely made up and zoe did this all for attention?" (ZoeQuinnText.txt, 2013). It seems as though there are people who will blame others for their own harassment no matter the type—although, to be fair, a troll could have set up this whole thing herself. It just simply was not the case. Eron comes into the channel later and talks as well.

Doc dumping, online, should *only* be performed if the document being dumped proves your case. Because ad-hocs have a lot of manpower, nearly any document can be pulled apart and searched for facts in a small amount of time. Doc dumping is a far better strategy in a law or political office where the amount of people who can possibly go through the evidence is fairly small.

Doc dumping can be dangerous though. Wikileaks has been both lauded and condemned for sharing classified information with the public. Free speech writ large can have damning effects upon politics and dangerous outcomes in the world. Doc dumping is *not* a neutral rhetorical act. Freedom of information is a rhetorical act that asks people to take action based upon that information. It can affect the outcomes of elections, the safety of government operatives, and relationships of countries and individuals around the world.

SWATTING

Swatting bears a lot in common with trolling that attempts to use the media against itself. However, instead of trying to get the news media to say something ridiculous or troll-related on the air, swatting attempts to exploit loopholes in the police force to try to get them to do something equally ridiculous (but even more dangerous). In swatting, a troll will call emergency services in the area that their target lives and attempt to get them to send out emergency vehicles—if not a SWAT team—to their target in hopes that the responders will be scary, disruptive, and even break down the door or arrest the target (Johansen, 2014). For example, in a video from someone live streaming themselves playing *Counter Strike*, a watching troll calls in a fake threat and the streamer is surrounded by cops holding machine guns, asked to put his hands up, and forced to lie on the ground. The casual description of this video on YouTube reads: "this happens sometimes."

This is done as a prank to many YouTubers, but also is done to people who are being otherwise harassed or attacked online. People at least attempted to send SWAT teams to the homes and offices of those who are opponents of GamerGate (Hern, 2015). For those with children or small animals, swatting can be a scary prospect.

Swatting would not be possible without overzealous police forces who often have military weapons, armor, and even vehicles. A police force with a tank is one that is probably more fun for trolls to manipulate than one without a tank.

Despite being potentially awful and terrifying, this is still a procedural trope (and, sadly, part of the current game). Anyone who wants to potentially learn how to place a call so that swatting occurs can easily find out online. However, swatting carries a high risk to the potential "player" who thinks it would be funny. Like many of these "current" techniques, swatting is illegal and dangerous. Not only could you be charged with a crime, but you could also potentially direct emergency services away from an accident, fire, or actual emergency.

Swatting is not just used by trolls, either. Some reports suggest that extreme liberals and conservatives alike are just as apt to use swatting as a technique to take down violent trolls or even pedophiles. However, even if used for "good" and despite being procedural and effective, swatting is dangerous, potentially deadly, and best avoided.

Many of the older procedural tropes used by ad-hocs are safer—not to say that they are not obnoxious or potentially financially threatening.

DELIVERIES

When I first read the PartyVan Wiki in the mid-2000s, sending many pizzas to the address of the doxxed individual was listed as a potential way to manipulate with targets. However, since this is a "classic" technique they also say that it is best to do something else since this is expected and many pizza parlors are aware of it (Insurgency Wiki, 2013).

However, then and now, many pizza shops (and larger chains) have started to allow people to place orders online and pay in person, even in small towns. This enables trolls to order pizzas and send them to doxxed addresses. Ideally, pizza is ordered from multiple shops rather than one hundred pizzas at once from one (which would be more likely to be flagged). Anons are encouraged to use a proxy server to hide their identity when placing an order (if they do not, their IP address might be revealed to the pizza shop and the person being targeted) (Insurgency Wiki, 2013). They might also make strange requests with the pizzas to manipulate their target. The wiki notes that in one case asking the shop to spell out a B in the pepperoni and deliver a message when the pizza was delivered convinced one target's mother that the pizza had been poisoned and she called the police.

An alternative to this technique is called a "box flood" (Insurgency Wiki, "Ruin Life Tactics," 2013). The United States Postal Service can deliver free boxes and other shipping products to peoples' homes. As a direct result, anybody with an address (and a fake email) can create an account and order lots of shipping products and have them sent to that address. Anons are directed to sites to create a free email account as part of the directions for this particular attack. One anon also, apparently, wrote a small program that sends boxes to a person continually via a loop. Anons have also been known to send purchase orders to companies, have products delivered to their target, and then hope that the target is sued by the company they sent the purchase order to (Insurgency Wiki, "Purchase Order," 2013).

In general, these techniques only work well if the sites do not require payment up front (or, alternately, if the anon in question does not mind spending money on trolling). Being doxxed opens up targets to these small annoyances as well as potential financial fraud, harassment of relatives, and swatting.

DDoS Attacks

A DDoS attack (distributed denial of service) occurs when a large number of computers are organized to all attempt to access a single website over and over again—all servers have a limit, and once that limit is reached the server cannot tell the difference between legitimate traffic and the DDoS attack and will fail and become inaccessible (Sauter, 2014). This is quite different from the previous procedural tropes listed above in that this is usually done to a website, not an individual, though it may cost individuals in lost income. DDoS attacks are also used as a form of protest, not just as a form of attack. In her book about DDoS attacks, Molly Sauter (2014) identifies them not only as a form of hacking (and potential illegal action—as many other writers do) but also as a form of civil disobedience. DDoS attacks online are important because they are one of the only ways that digital protestors have to gain an audience. As noted in a foreword to the book written by Ethan Zuckerman, these are usually seen as a "bad thing" as they violate some of the basic principles of freedom of speech by completely silencing a target for a period of time (Sauter, 2014). While DDoS attacks are recognized as less "ethically neat" than other forms of dissent that are already widely practiced, Sauter identifies them as a way that users of the Internet can create public space in which to dissent.

Despite early hopes that the Internet would be a wonderful place for public debate and dissent—for the most part that hasn't happened. Sites are owned by private entities and the speech allowed on them is moderated tightly (in this light, 4Chan and sites like it are unique for their enacting of the public space). You can, of course, make your own site to protect another one—but getting an audience is increasingly difficult. In short, in a place where everyone can speak, it can be difficult to be heard (Zuckerman, in Sauter, 2014). If we are all allowed to speak but no one can hear us, that does little to create a free society. In short, Sauter sees taking over or taking down another company or organization's website is one way that you can gain an audience who will listen to you. DDoS attacks force attention and can be used to change the way that

> The overwhelmingly privatized nature of the internet is a challenge to the practice of activism online, on the levels of large-scale peaceable assembly, freedom of expression, and civil disobedience. Early practitioners of DDoS actions recognized this, and staged their actions, in part, with the goal of legitimating, through practice, civil disobedience online. (Sauter, 2014, loc. 178–80)

However, our current cultural "script" for civil disobedience simply does not take these actions into account.

Our modern-day sense of what civil disobedience is, says Sauter (2014), was built in the 1950s and 1960s, heavily publicized, and has become iconic. Civil disobedience looks like street marches, refusing to move on the bus, and having lunch-counter sit-ins. Media that cover such events legitimize that they are political (Sauter, 2014). But when looking at DDoS attacks, rarely are they legitimized in the media. Instead, if they are published about at all, we find out about the legal consequences of taking down Starbucks' website for an afternoon (during which time everyone could still buy coffee).

DDoS attacks are often seen as lazy because people do not have to leave their homes and participate in the way that Rosa Parks, Martin Luther King Jr., and others before them did—people performing them are called "slacktivists," for example. But in this new online space, there isn't any space to protest in that would be effective *other* than what they are already doing. Replacing the text on a page (another technique, though not as common as it used to be) through a redirect or performing a DDoS attack interferes enough with the normal flow of business that it gets attention in a way that a separate protest site will not.

Sauter describes the difference between older civil disobedience and newer, digital civil disobedience as:

> The storytelling which occurs around social movements favors clear, emotionally compelling through-lines, which are often difficult, if not impossible to discern in the moment, on the street, or at the computer. The present is always messy, only the past has the opportunity to be clean(ed). Ongoing or developing activist actions simply cannot be consumed by the public in the same fashion as iconic social movements which have had half a century to establish narratives in the media and the public imagination. Criticism that compares the developing world of online-based activism, such as DDoS actions or "clicktavist" or "slacktivist" actions, to the sit-ins and boycotts of the Civil Rights Movement is essentially empty. Not only do these new movements and actions not have the same goals as the Civil Rights Movement, they are also not organized by activists with the same level of or same kind of experience, and they occupy entirely different historical moments, with respect to when they are taking place, when they are being examined, and how. So not only do these popular critiques often bear little relationship to how the Civil Rights Movement occurred on the ground, but they also fail to realize that a comparison between internet-based activism occurring at the turn of the millennium and the iconic ideal of the midcentury Civil Rights Movement often serves no other purpose than to fault the current generation of political activists for not being their grandparents. (Sauter, 2014, loc. 541–51)

We also tend to ignore the less "pretty" forms of civil disobedience that were popular in the past when we celebrate the Civil Rights Movement—it wasn't all peaceful sit-ins. Disruptive activism has always existed, and DDoS attacks are just one example of a new form of it.

It could be argued that DDoS attacks are meaningless as the site attacked obviously cannot host content while it is being attacked. The site goes down, the hackers win, and—what? How do you find out what they were protesting to begin with?

According to Sauter (2014), the "signal disruption" caused by the site going down could be considered content in and of itself. However, there are techniques (many of which were pioneered by Anonymous, and others by EDT—a group that called themselves Electronic Disturbance Theater) that ensure that the "signal" beyond the DDoS attack itself will be heard. DDoS attacks must be calibrated, then, alongside other manipulation of the media such as creation of videos, distribution of memes, and broadcasting of images. Anonymous has become quite good at getting these videos put on broadcast television—mostly through higher production quality (and not to mention how startlingly eerie it is to be spoken to by a distorted voice in a Guy Fawkes' mask). Because they have the ability to create and disseminate media quickly they have an advantage in using DDoS attacks to broadcast the rest of their message to the entire world via manipulating the mass media in a way that many smaller groups simply do not.

However, some people will always see DDoS attacks as controversial because they are a form of censorship. Organizing a DDoS attack (even if done by software, it is most effective if many people are involved) means that you are silencing someone or something. By this view, a DDoS attack is "wrong" no matter what its purpose because it stops the free flow of information online. Someone wanted to go to that site, and they have the right to that information—and anyone choosing to take that right away is censoring the web.

WHITE TEXTING

One of the strangest tropes that I have found used rarely but very well when employed is one I call "white texting." In white texting, information about a person is hidden on a website or in a document within text that is the same color as the background. This trick is sometimes used by job seekers who want to hide a bunch of keywords at the bottom of their resume, and was also on some websites for search engine optimization purposes. However, those techniques have largely died out as search engine indexing got smarter—and so did the people reviewing resumes after a computer got done with them. Still, white texting can be a powerful tool to make a statement about someone that the person cannot see, but computers can. A white texted message will show up in search results but be difficult for the person it is about to find, for example.

White texting is not commonly used by Anonymous or 4Chan, but has been used by other organizations. The most interesting example I have found online involves the organization "Autism Speaks." Now, Autism Speaks is controversial to begin with because many people that have autism do not support it—they don't see themselves as something that needs to be "fixed" or a puzzle piece that needs to be fit back into the puzzle. One member of the autistic community online whose screenname is Kassiane found herself quoted in one of their transition kits without permission, and they cited her incorrectly (her quote appeared in a book and permission had not been granted by the publisher) (Hillary, 2014).

A full year after she asked for the material to be removed, someone else noticed that if you searched for the text it was still present—just invisible. In this way, the organization was able to continue using her quote and would have it show up in their Google Search results, but they did not have to properly attribute it. Furthermore, the writer (who does not wish to be associated with Autism Speaks) now has a search result that shows up when you search her name with their organization's name (Hillary, 2014). It is also claimed that the quote was removed for a while and returned later—suggesting that they did intend to put it back up after some time had passed.

White texting allows all sorts of organizations, ad-hocracies, and individuals to hide information in plain sight and, therefore, is one of the easier procedural tropes that could be followed. However, if it is found it can certainly disrupt the ethos of its source.

Tl;dr

The tl;dr (stands for "too long; didn't read) is a procedure designed to dismiss arguments that the reader does not like providing that they are long. While it may have started as a way to suggest that an argument was too long to be read on a screen (or just too long period), it has developed in two ways.

1.   It is used as a dismissal similar to the *argumentum ad lapidem*—a fallacy wherein an argument is dismissed as ridiculous without saying why it is ridiculous (Alexander, 1923).

2.   Rhetors summarize their own arguments at the beginning or end at some communities (such as Reddit) with a tl;dr. After posting a long story they will skip a line, type "tl;dr" (and sometimes bold it) and write a very brief summary of the main parts, thus keeping anyone else from complaining that their original text was too long.

In the first case, tl;dr can be used against an argument of any length. Claiming "tl;dr" on a short argument, for example, suggests that even a few short phrases are too time-consuming to bother with reading. On longer posts it might be used to accuse someone of being long winded, a poor writer, or of simply having a different viewpoint. Its similarity to *argumentum ad lapidem* stems from it being a dismissal for dismissal's sake—this is too long, and therefore ridiculous, so I will not read it to find out what it has to say.

The second is fairly self-explanatory, but has spawned a technique similar to doc dumping as well. Called *argumentum ad tl;dr*, the rhetor intentionally and procedurally writes a long winded argument that they do not intend anyone to ever read (RationalWiki, 2015). It likely contains long diversions that have absolutely nothing to do with the topic at hand to hide the fact that the argument itself is fairly weak. As such it also shares rhetorical roots with the filibuster.

Unlike other procedures discussed, tl;dr can be used as a trope either by the person attacking a viewpoint or defending it. It is, at the moment, a versatile and recognizable tool (though will likely fall out of style within the next decade). As noted before, short and pithy arguments are valued on the Internet, and the tl;dr is a reflection of that. However, we cannot afford to misrecognize the power of a short statement. Several recent studies have shown that Twitter—limited, for now, to 140 characters—can be immensely powerful *because* it is not meant to carry large messages. For example, a study by Solow-Niedermann (2010) showed that Twitter can be used in an authoritarian state (in the case of Iran's elections) to disseminate information. Unfortunately, she also found that Twitter is not a good tool for mobilizing people. Despite that, forcing people to shrink their arguments to their most essential parts has long been an exercise in writing classrooms and now has gained power and popularity online as well.

SOCKPUPPETS

I noted earlier that when a person is banned from a site they are generally able to make a new account. When users make new accounts (in addition to their existing one), especially when they make many new accounts, that is called creating a sockpuppet. Sockpuppets were named such because, like puppets made of socks, they are simple to create, can be turned into anything at all, and also mimic the person who made them.

Sockpuppets are useful. If you want someone to back you up and agree that your argument is worthwhile, making a second account allows you to do that *without* having to convince another human being that you are correct. You can also use a sockpuppet to start a fight with yourself, and make the other person you are "fighting" with look like the most horrible representative of the group they are arguing from possible. With a sockpuppet, it is easy to make a man-hating feminist or a deeply misogynistic men's rights activist—you don't have to wait for one to come around, you can simply play one yourself.

In some cases, individuals have created hundreds of sockpuppets from which to argue. In many forums this behavior is against the rules and will lead to IP address bans that are meant to keep people from creating new accounts. However, savvy users will know how to spoof their IP, so this is not terribly effective.

Interestingly enough, the US Government and military have been creating sockpuppets in some forums to spread "pro-American propaganda" (Fielding & Cobain, 2011). According to an article in the *Guardian*, the military is investigating software that would allow it to manipulate social media sites and post pro-American memes and messages (that will then be reposted by real people). The software developed is meant to also target foreign-language websites that create anti-American sentiment in a hope to improve the message that people in those countries receive about the United States (Fielding & Cobain, 2011). There is concern that, in the future, both other countries and private companies will gain access to this software or develop their own to insert propaganda into our existing social media networks.

HASHTAG ON TWITTER

Creating a popular hashtag on Twitter is a good way to encourage people to participate in a cause or gain recognition for an event. A hashtag is a word (or bunch of words squished together) used to label Twitter (or Instagram or Facebook) posts. You can search for hashtags to view lists of all of the tweets that currently are discussing a subject. Furthermore, Twitter keeps metrics of hashtags that are currently "trending" and shows these on its main page. Viewing what is currently trending will give Twitter users a quick idea of what campaigns are currently popular and encourage them to join. They are often used to share experiences and advertise products as well (and some companies do better than others at this).

Many of the previous attacks that I have discussed were backed up with Twitter campaigns as well. #Gamergate had a lot of activity on Twitter, with dissenters attempting to create their own anti-GamerGate tags (like "GameOverGate"). Many of these campaigns had real-world counterparts. #OccupyWallStreet had a successful Twitter hashtag, as did #BlackLivesMatter in the days (and now months and years) after Michael Brown was killed by a police officer in Ferguson, Missouri.

What is perhaps most powerful about having a nationally trending hashtag (other than exposure in general) is that it simply isn't that difficult for a tag to trend nationally. In 2013, the Computers & Writing hashtag (#cwcon) briefly trended nationally, as was announced at one of our meals. With about 380 total conference participants (between registered attendees and workers), and not all of them actively using Twitter, the hashtag "made it," so to speak, to brief national prominence. Of course, Computers and Writing attendees tend to be both very technologically savvy and good writers (as well as loquacious), so it is within the realm of possibility that a similarly sized group of less active users or users who know less about writing would not be able to perform the same feat. However, at the very least, this type of procedure seems *possible* for the average ad-hoc to perform.

REPHRASING/FIXED THAT FOR YOU

On message boards (both anonymous and not), it is not uncommon to see someone repost someone else's reply or post, cross-out or change a word or two, and post "Fixed that for you" or "FTFY" as a response.

This sarcastic means of dismissal turns the original post into a joke and, according to Urban Dictionary, sarcastically disagrees at the same time (2015).

This type of rephrasing derails the initial conversation with humor, and may also be meant to somewhat humiliate the original poster (OP). This is also used successfully in many places because it reminds the original poster of being corrected in school. Imitating teachers, it seems, is one popular procedural trope (that may also damage the credibility of teachers when they do the same).

NUMBERS AS RHETORICAL DEVICE

In an ad-hoc, sheer numbers carry a lot of power. Having many members of an ad-hoc all performing the same activity at once is powerful enough to drop a web server, and it is also possible that they can overwhelm an argument.

If one person is fighting against an entire army (or more if the army contains sockpuppets), their chances of surviving or winning are very slim. One of the most common procedural tropes is simply to throw numbers at a problem. One hundred people posting all at once drowns out whatever original argument was being made, and can also be frightening to the person receiving the replies and messages.

Numbers can also be used to keep messages coming all day and night for an extended period of time, which is why they are also a powerful procedure. While a single individual can, maybe, make a difference online, they are very unlikely to be able to do so in the face of a swarm. Thus, the best way to guard against a hoard of attackers who all use the name "anonymous" is probably going to be to have a swarm of your own. This is where individuals that are being attacked fail—and it's also where many companies fail as well. A single Twitter account belonging to a corporation is not going to be able to stop or block a Twitter protest because they cannot possibly respond often enough to be effective. Indeed, the entire PR team of many major corporations would struggle. The best bet for a corporation undergoing a swarmed attack would be to appeal to customers to defend them—so if the customers are who is swarming, or customers who have little loyalty, companies are left with little recourse except through the law.

Rick-Rolling/Redirecting

One of the less destructive procedural tools is redirecting. People are encouraged to click on a link to watch a video, listen to music, or read about one topic and then end up seeing something else entirely. When I was a college student, it was not uncommon to redirect people to Goatse or Tubgirl—two gross images which shall not be recreated here. Friends enjoyed getting friends to go look at one of these images as part of a trick.

Redirecting works on the same principle. You have your target click on a link to find out more about something they are interested in, and they are taken to a video of Rick Astley singing "Never Gonna Give You Up" (something that is called Rick Rolling). Astley is a good sport—he even appeared on a Thanksgiving Day parade float to perform the song as a sort of live Rickroll gift to the world for the holidays.

Redirecting wastes time and energy of the target and sometimes makes them angry, but is mostly just good clean fun. It can be used maliciously to point users towards illegal or dangerous content, but usually points towards obnoxious or overused content instead of anything dangerous.

Anti-Trolling

I have briefly discussed anti-trolling in past chapters. Specifically, I discussed Oisín Sweeney and his book *Hackers on Steroids* (2013). Sweeny is an "anti-troll." He uses trolling techniques to fight back against trolls that he particularly finds malevolent—specifically pedophiles and RIP trolls. Sweeney explains the reasons behind his trolling of trolls as such:

> Many, many users of the Internet really . . . deserve to be winded up. . . . By creating different personas and adopting satirical positions in extreme opposition to their own and yet simultaneously using their own hypocrisies against them, I have, over the years, made all of these types of buffoon and more explode with anger and dedicate post after post of real hatred towards me on forums and I have cried genuine tears of laughter at it when it has happened. So I have trolled. I have been a troll. I think trolling, when done right, is great fun. (Sweeney, 2013, loc. 194)

Anti-trolls will use techniques from trolls—even doxxing, doc dumping, and DDoS attacks—to expose trolls that they believe have stepped over some boundary or another.

For example, Sweeney was able to determine the real-life identity of one of the RIP trolls that he had been following and accused him of being a pedophile. Sweeney sees no problem with doing this to someone who is an RIP troll—it almost seems as if he sees threatening men with pedophilia as a "worst possible thing" equivalent to threatening women with rape:

> after satisfying myself that he was the troll I took all of his details—from his small town to his two email addresses—and made a page outing him as someone who happily boasts of his sexual appetite for children. The link to my open page I then spammed all over any Facebook group I could find related to his home town. Maybe he has a real sexual appetite for children, maybe he doesn't. But that's what he claimed on the countless RIP pages he attacked, and if it was a joke then I wasn't laughing. I didn't label him as a paedophile, just simply crucified him with his own nails. (Sweeney, 2013, loc. 380–406)

Sweeney was ultimately successful in shutting down the trolls that he wanted to stop. Turning trolling techniques on the trolls can be tempting I'm sure, but not only can it turn you into a bitter troll yourself, but it can also turn out very badly if you upset the wrong people.

Jennifer Emick knows this all too well, as she has been one of the targets of Anonymous after first being a member (Biddle, 2012). Emick is a forty-something mother who once outed another troll (by doxxing him). As a result, she has been a target of Anonymous.

I've said elsewhere that Anonymous mostly now targets groups— but they can certainly turn against people who they feel have wronged them. In this case, Emick is an anti-troll (Biddle, 2012). Emick started off as a member of Project Chanology—she was writing articles about Scientology for About.com after she had family problems with the religion. Despite enjoying these protests she didn't see a clear direction that Anonymous was following—they were split between wanting to deal with privacy issues, Wikileaks, and simply going back to their roots of harassing individuals (Biddle, 2012). Since she wanted to continue to make money from her involvement in Anonymous, she decided to create a company (Backtrace Security) that collects insider information to use in cases against Anonymous (and likely other online ad-hocs like it).

Needless to say, Anonymous did not applaud her decision to make money off of being an anti-troll. Her business and personal life were instantly under every attack and harassment that trolls generally use, including doxxing, threats to herself, and threats to her family. They have also threatened to put her children's photos on a pedophile website (Biddle, 2012). The cost of being an anti-troll might be high. Using trolling and hacking techniques against trolls and hackers might seem like a natural fit, but anyone interested should understand that the price could be great. Getting sucked into trolling has not made Sweeney more empathetic (unless the book itself is a troll), and Emick has had her life turned upside down by her venture into outing hackers to the government.

ASKING FOR SOURCES

The next trope I will discuss in this chapter seems innocuous as it is something we do as teachers all the time. However, that does not change the fact that one of the surest ways to attempt to discredit another person online is simply to ask for sources. Yes, asking for a citation is an offensive procedural rhetorical trope.

For example, when asked what was one of the worst things that users see on Reddit, being asked for sources was one of the most up-voted comments. Being asked for sources suggested that your personal opinion and experience is invalid. Being asked for additional sources suggests that the troll in question will accept nothing less than a double-blind study of several thousand people. I've posted links to many studies in the past, and none of them are "good enough" proof if someone is asking you for a source. From Reddit:

> Reddit takes it *way* too far when asking for citations. Yes, if you don't know or don't believe, by all means, expand your knowledge, and good on you for asking, but for the love of god, use some . . . common sense first. . . . If I say that Australia has a land area of 7.7 million km^2, don't ask for a source, because this is what happens when you Google "Australia." Chances are, it'll be quicker than waiting for a reply anyway. (UnholyDemigod, 2012)

Additionally, in the same thread, Redditors call for each other to stop being hostile when someone makes a grammar mistake.

Both of these are ultimately seen as part of the "logical" troll. Trolls are logical, smart, and nerdy—and part of being those things is being able to cite sources, spell, and use grammar properly. Suggesting that someone is stupid by correcting their grammar or asking for citations is a common way to discredit a person that you don't agree with. If these tools were *not* used primarily in cases where one person wishes to discredit another (trolls rarely correct the grammar and spelling of other trolls, recognizing that many misspellings in troll posts are just part of trolling), then they probably would not be nearly so offensive. Redditors also pointed out that many users of the site are non-native speakers and therefore should not be put under the scrutiny that they are for their grammar and spelling:

> If someone makes a spelling or grammar error, correct them, but in a *non-hostile way*. There are millions of subscribers to this site. For many of them, English is not their first language. And in the case of people who have English as a first language, people make mistakes. (UnholyDemigod, 2012)

CopyPasta

One of the simplest and most effective means of procedural persuasion that is used by ad-hocs is "CopyPasta"—phrases, sentences, and paragraphs that are copied and pasted over and over again at a target. A single argument, then, can be copied and pasted by hundreds or thousands of anons and delivered to one or many targets. In this way, the anons do not have to come up with their own material—they simply deliver the CopyPasta.

They are unconcerned with plagiarism, in this case, though no doubt would accuse others for plagiarism if they found such repeated phrases in the writing of their enemies. CopyPasta reduces rhetoric to its most simplistic and procedural parts—copy and paste this phrase, that's all you have to do in order to be "rhetorically effective."

Of course, without numbers, this would not be effective. Furthermore, since many of the things being repeated are memes and catch-phrases of the group, it should be of little surprise that those are what is often copied and pasted.

MEMES AND OTHER REPETITIVE PHRASES

I have already discussed memes as one of the cornerstones of online ad-hocracies. Memes help build ad-hocs. They create community, and help rapidly create a shared discourse community. When used outside that community, however, they can be used as a procedurally rhetorical attack.

In the logs I have of deleted messages from 4Chan and Anonymous (BB) and the chat log from GamerGate, some of the slang (raep) and memes known to be used by these groups are repeated time and again. To an outsider, these seem rude, accusatory, or just plain crazy. But this is a way that ad-hocs mark their territory. They use this language to be exclusionary and keep out anyone who isn't part of their group. They are intentionally baiting people to ask "Wtf?" or get upset at the things they post, all of which are memes and slang from within their own groups.

The best example of this is, of course, Oprah Winfrey saying "nine thousand penises" on air. Oprah and her writers (who should have known enough to do their research) did not realize that this was a meme, and that by saying it on air the trolls won. "Over nine thousand" was a reference to a *Dragonball Z* episode (Phillips, 2015), while joking about child pornography became popular through the ironic mascot "Pedobear." Pedobear tends to be used mockingly—to suggest that others are interested in child pornography, or as a dark mascot of everything that is wrong with childhood today. Regardless, the meme—"innocent" enough in its own right—was used as an attack against an opponent who did not know what it meant.

The best defense against having memes used against you (or not recognizing them) is to take the time to be aware of what is popular. Much as you understand television and movie references if you actually watch television and movies, memes have to be studied to be understood.

CONCLUSION

Many of the tropes listed in this chapter as being procedural are terrifying—I know that. I know that many members of my audience are saying, "Why would anyone want to persuade this way?" In many ways, I agree with those people.

In chapter 5, I will be covering the rhetorical understructure that trolls and ad-hocs use online to persuade procedurally. However, *that does not mean that doxxing, DDoS attacks, and Swatting are not part of their game.* I do not feel that it would be valid or fair to discuss these specific ad-hocs without also discussing the very real ways in which they are terrifying and wield massive amounts of power.

Trolls' procedural rhetorics are as effective as they are because they are backed up with what amounts to deadly force. While some of these techniques are deeply researched (by the trolls) and others are rhetorically viable on their own, they work as well as they do because people online know that if you upset the wrong person you will end up doxxed or worse. Therefore most, if not all, of them still fall under fallacies and can only be seen as rhetorical when they are viewed through games and proceduralism.

5 Procedural Rhetorical Tropes and Memes

INTRODUCTION

The last chapter focused on the procedures used in the Game of the Internet that are based in action, creation, and perhaps even real work or network-based action. This chapter focuses on the linguistic and lexical tropes that build procedural rhetorics.

Trolls are not a-rhetorical. In some cases they have studied famous rhetoricians such as Plato and Aristotle, and some even recognize Socrates as the first troll. Others familiarize themselves with the work of Arthur Schopenhauer (2013) to learn to employ rhetoric and fallacies in online arguments. They are not, at the end of the day, unaware of traditional rhetorical tropes, but instead reject them for what they see works—sophistic and procedural rhetoric, sarcasm, and fallacies. Their procedures, while systematic, are based upon the work of the great rhetoricians that came before.

THIS IS WHY WE CAN'T HAVE NICE THINGS

In her book *This is Why We Can't Have Nice Things*, Whitney Phillips (2015) has a lot to say about trolls and people who play on the Internet. Most importantly, she is one of the first theorists who takes a solid look at the rhetoric of play on trolling communities. She notes that trolling and play "is, or at least can be, an extremely effective rhetorical strategy" (p. 159). Like traditional rhetoric, the type of procedural rhetoric that the Game of the Internet follows "[snaps] its audience to attention" (2015, p. 159) by bringing up topics that they are emotionally invested in. Trolling rhetoric might also make a claim so outrageous that the person responding feels like they have to respond. These techniques are cribbed, in part, from the work of Arthur Schopenhauer (2013). Trolling also tends to attempt to draw out what a target really thinks. The point of the game is to get the target to admit that they have faults, prejudices, and problems too—and then the troll will use these admissions against the initial target. This is manipulative and exploitative, but that doesn't mean that it isn't a sound procedural principle. The means by which this is done are almost entirely systematic and methodical: All of your carefully held beliefs will be used against you. If it can be named, it can be hated.

Trolls also proceduralize the best ways to respond—if the target says X do Y in response. Phillips (2015) argues that "arguments imbued with trolling rhetoric have the potential to open avenues of discourse that wouldn't have been possible otherwise, either because the conversation never would have arisen or because the participants wouldn't have felt compelled to respond even if it had" (p. 160). She sees the potential for this kind of discourse to start conversations that we would not be having otherwise, as well as its ability to highlight problems in the media and problems in the ways that we treat minorities. For example, trolls use slang and awful, terrible, no-good language all the time—but the way in which they do it highlights the ways in which all white people misappropriate and use these words. Take their use of the n-word. It's possible to see the way that white people use the term (in private, hidden, amongst friends, as their dirty little secret) being made fun of in the completely open and ridiculous use of the term in trolling. Of course, very problematically, this also covers up times when it is used seriously.

Phillips (2015) also sees trolling rhetoric (or procedural rhetoric) as the only means of effectively countering trolls. When I began to study this type of rhetoric, especially as a game, my initial goal was to create means by which people could fight back. While I can highlight common strategies that are being used in the moment, right now, to proceduralize rhetoric online, I cannot predict what will be done two or three years from now, let alone ten or twenty. Thus, those specific strategies lack the staying power of traditional rhetoric.

Procedural rhetorics in trolling spaces are ephemeral and ever-changing. The primary means by which they can be guarded against and countered is by studying them. What is popular now? What techniques are most effective in the present? What can be done to use the language and techniques of this group in the present against themselves if they become problematic? Those are the questions that we should be looking at if we want to teach these types of procedures.

In countering trolls, Phillips also directly calls out trolling as a game:

> Actively trolling trolls . . . runs directly counter to the common
> imperative "don't feed the trolls," a statement predicated on the
> logic that trolls can only troll if their targets allow themselves to
> be trolled. Given that the fun of trolling inheres in the game of
> trolling—a game only the troll can win, and whose rules only
> the troll can modify—this is sound advice. If the target doesn't
> react, then neither can the troll. But even this decision buys into
> the trolls' game. The troll still sets the terms of their target's en-
> gagement; the troll still controls the timeline and the outcome.
> The dynamic shifts considerably if the target counters with a
> second game, one that collapses the boundary between target
> and troll. In this new game, the troll can lose and, by taking
> umbrage at the possibility, falls victim to his or her own rigid
> rules. After all, it's emotion—particularly frustration or dis-
> tress—that trips the troll's wire. In most cases, the troll's shame
> over having lost, or merely the possibility that he or she could
> lose, will often send the troll searching for more exploitable pas-
> tures. (Phillips, 2015, pp. 160–61)

In this quote there are at least two points worth noting: (1) She recognizes trolling as a kind of rhetorical play and (2) she also recognizes that
by trolling a troll you are creating a new game.

In other parts of this text I have briefly argued that in the Game of
the Internet the audience determines the winning condition. In what
Phillips describes, targets can create games of their own. Don't like the
rules of the game you are playing? Play another game. She suggests that
anyone attacked let trolls know that they are aware of the game and
that they know how to play—you do this by engaging and disrupting
the play and turning it into a different argument. The game is meant to
"disrupt and upset as many people as possible, using whatever linguistic
or behavioral tools are available" as if the troll were a suddenly ultra-
aggressive Aristotle bent on world domination by rhetoric (persuasion
by any means available = persuasion by whatever tools or procedures are
available) (2015, p. 2).

Like many androcentric rhetors, trolls privilege "cool rationality over
emotionalism," and equate the act of "exerting dominance over a given
adversary" with "winning," which also speaks to their viewing rhetoric
as a (procedural) game (Phillips, 2015, p. 124). They see the androcen-

tric nature of their rhetoric as necessary, as logic is better than emotion in every way. They apply the "adversary method" of philosophy, a term coined by Janice Moulton (1983) to describe how being "cool, calm, and unflinchingly rational; to forward specific claims; and to check those claims against potential counterarguments, all in the service of defeating or otherwise outmaneuvering one's opponent(s)" is preferable over other forms of argumentation (Phillips, 2015, p. 124). Though trolls might phrase it as "knowing how to rhetoric" and take this as a point of great pride, it is also how they explain away their worst behaviors. Logic and rationalism are better than emotion, so if what they do is both logical and rational and meant to get an emotional rise out of someone else, then they aren't just being jerks, they are also being teachers (see that they also correct grammar and ask for sources). They are helping the "other" learn "how to rhetoric" better by their own example. Yes, this behavior is inherently sexist and often linguistically and socially violent, but it is also culturally engrained as a type of pedagogy, even if it is one that real professors try to move against.

THE MEDIA CYCLE

Ultimately, Whitney Phillips (2015) argues that trolls are not the problem (or they are not the entire problem). I might even argue that trolls are not a problem, at least not when they focus on being rhetorically different and provocative instead of sending SWAT teams to random peoples' homes.

Although many people have claimed otherwise, trolls and their style of harassment alone are not what is "wrong" with the Internet, nor are they the reason we "can't have nice things." An article published in 2015 that claims that Twitter is dying because of harassment and insularity argues that companies like Twitter's inability or disinterest in stopping harassment when faced with how that would hurt their ad revenue are the problem (Haque, 2015). Unfortunately, what this and other articles like it fail to recognize is that the same spaces that breed harassment also breed creativity, and therefore we should look at what starts the harassment without attempting to stall the creativity.

This makes Phillips' argument particularly attractive. She argues that trolls, " . . . are born of and embedded within dominant institutions and tropes, which are every bit as damaging as the trolls' most disruptive behaviors. Ultimately, then, this is why we can't have nice things, and is the point to which the title gestures: the fact that online trolling is par for the mainstream cultural course" (2015, p. 11). For example, trolls know that they can potentially get the media to say extremely gross things on the air because of the shock value of that content (and shock value sells ads). Phillips uses the example of "Jenkem," a story that trolls got into the American media. Jenkem is a drug created by fermenting human waste in jars (use your imagination here) in the sun and then inhaling the fumes to get high. Trolls managed to convince the media that this was popular in American schools. This is their way of highlighting "look at how stupid the media is." By manipulating the news cycle and discussing how to insert themselves into it, trolls highlight exactly what is wrong with our news and media. It should not be so easy to manipulate, and it *breeds* trolls. Trolls are an "implicit critique of the ways in which media research and report the news" (Phillips, 2015, p. 6). Even if individual trolls do not wish to critique the media, by exploiting it, that critique occurs. If we learn nothing else from this, it is that we must teach budding journalist students about the ways that the media cycle can be perverted not just by trolls but by corporations and private individuals so that it becomes more honest and less driven by extremism.

Phillips also argues that the racism that is present in our media is more toxic than that which is presented by trolls. The media is the essential trigger from which a lot of people learn that racism is essentially culturally relevant. Trolls play off of cultural relevance. They also often don't mean what they say—they divorce themselves from their "mask of trolling," and will post the worst possible thing which is usually racism or a threat. By saying that they are "just trolling" (with echoes of "just gaming"), they get complete control over how much their trolling matches their personal beliefs. Even so, trolls use rhetoric and what they know of psychology to determine exactly how their behaviors affect others and pinpoint which issues and procedures will affect their targets the most. Phillips quotes one troll (Wilson Mouzone) who stated, "[Great trolls] fully understand the implications of everything they say and do, and that's what makes them great trolls. They have empathy and can work out the best way to wind people up, but that also means they are fully aware of the harm they cause" (as quoted in Phillips, 2015, pp. 35–36). Ultimately, too, trolls that completely lack empathy and cannot figure out how to get to people will not be successful trolls. This empathy can be put towards other (rhetorical) means.

Can There be a Feminist Trolling "Turn"?

Can there be a feminist troll? In an article in the *Fembot Collective* written by Amanda Phillips (2012), lessons taught by trolls and harassers are certainly able to be used for feminist purposes. Since trolling is culturally pervasive and is everywhere we are (not just online, but in person as well), it would be in the best interest of feminists and generally everyone to learn how it works and to defend against it.

Like real trolls, feminist trolls can encourage misogynists and racists to keep talking, and to get them to eventually speak their true ideas (rather than whatever watered down ones they usually share publically). This can confuse them and make them angry, of course, but it is a valid technique in getting them to expose themselves (Phillips, 2015). Unfortunately, this technique has lost some relevancy in the rise of Donald Trump as a politician. His "truth," especially delivered by Twitter and in older recordings, does not seem to be watered down at all—and his constituents appreciate that truth, even when it contains ableism or racism. Whether or not such "truth" becomes common again in American discourse remains to be seen.

Phillips (2015) ends her discussion of trolling rhetoric by noting that while it may be nice to turn trolling rhetoric around and use it on the trolls, it doesn't always speak well when

> those invested in an anti-oppression framework engage in behaviors that are fundamentally asymmetrical, that actively seek to dominate and publicly humiliate one's opponent, and that, most problematically, preclude consent. Just as Audre Lorde warned against using patriarchal rhetoric, patriarchal structures of organization, and patriarchal privileging of solidarity over difference to dismantle patriarchy, I too am reluctant to wholeheartedly claim for the feminist cause a rhetorical mode so thoroughly steeped in male domination. On the other hand, if the goal is to dismantle patriarchal structures, and if feminist trolling helps accomplish those ends, then are the means, however problematic, retroactively justified? (Phillips, 2015, pp. 167–68)

In short, there's no easy answer to whether anti-trolling can or should be a feminist or anti-racist goal, but it *might* be successful, especially as a means of last resort. The feminist or anti-racist who wishes to take a stand online should, at the least, familiarize themselves with the means of persuasion used in those spaces. As such, in addition to looking at the procedures in the previous chapter, here we will examine the more traditional rhetorics and classical writings upon which trolling has been built.

THE ART OF CONTROVERSY

Trolls have adopted the work of Arthur Schopenhauer, a nineteenth-century philosopher, as one way of "learning how to rhetoric." His *The Art of Controversy* (original 1896, my copy 2013) is a collection of essays meant to tell the modern rhetor how to deal with any number of rhetorical situations in the most expedient (though perhaps not classical) means possible, often through the use of fallacy. Unsurprisingly, trolls see this as a "blueprint for modern trolling" (Phillips, 2015, p. 124). The book sees defeating an opponent as winning, and it may be done by doing things like forcing an opponent's claim so far beyond its natural limits that the opponent has no choice but to agree that that form (a straw man) is indeed part of his claim. That extreme argument can then be brought down by a simple series of counterarguments. This is called "the Extension," which

> consists in carrying your opponent's proposition beyond its natural limits; in giving it as general a signification and as wide a sense as possible, so as to exaggerate it; and, on the other hand, in giving your own proposition as restricted a sense and as narrow limits as you can, because the more general a statement becomes, the more numerous are the objections to which it is open. The defense consists in an accurate statement of the point or essential question at issue. (Schopenhauer, 2013, p. 3)

Schopenhauer also points out that making an opponent angry is a good way to make them unable to argue effectively. His work is, in short, a complete guide written over a century ago that explains how to troll and why trolling works.

In another technique, "The Homonymy," the troll is told:

> to extend a proposition to something which has little or nothing in common with the matter in question but the similarity of the word; then to refute it triumphantly, and so claim credit for having refuted the original statement. (Schopenhauer, 2013, p. 4)

For example, Schopenhauer says that if an opponent states something to the effect of "you do not yet understand the mysteries of rhetoric" then the opponent can state that they will have nothing to do with mysteries, as if their problem with the word *mysteries* is the entirety of the argument, thus ending an entire discussion that had nothing to do with mysteries to begin with. I have seen this technique used not only by trolls, but also by academics on Facebook and popular list-servs.

Another trick that Schopenhauer writes about is to find one very small place in which an argument is wrong. For example, the argument is made that cats are quite furry. To use this trick, the opponent would say that the inside of cats' mouths are not furry, so that cats are both furry and not at the same time. This is an "obvious sophism," but if it keeps the opponent off-centered and confused it may help to make them angry (Schopenhauer, 2013, p. 6). He also recommends that instead of drawing a conclusion, the rhetor must hide that conclusion, if at all possible, and get the opponent to agree to several premises beforehand (Socrates, of course, does this often in Plato's dialogues). Those premises should then be mingled into the overall rhetoric of a piece so that the opponent will not feel like they are giving up anything when they agree with them.

Alternately, if the opponent will not agree with the premises, "you must advance the premises of these premises; that is to say, you must draw up pro-syllogisms, and get the premises of several of them admitted in no definite order. In this way, you conceal your game until you have obtained all the admissions that are necessary, and so reach your goal by making a circuit" (Schopenhauer, 2013, p. 7). If a person is a member of a group—say, they are a feminist—you may use the beliefs of that group against the feminist. This is especially effective against feminism since feminism does not represent a solid, unified group with solid, unified positions. The nature of today's feminism means that one can use a sex-negative position against a sex-positive feminist and claim that their own position is not feminism fairly easily (this is a move I see repeated often on Reddit). One of his later techniques also suggests that you can mix in throwing an aspersion onto a comment by claiming that it belongs to a group that you can assume that your audience either does not like or would be embarrassed to be called a part of (or, alternately, happy to be a part of but feel stupid for having it explained to them as if they were young). For example, they might call something capitalism or communism. Most recently, after explaining what cultural appropriation was on

Reddit I was told by another poster that that was just "capitalism" and therefore not only perfectly alright but also American. Schopenhauer's definition only includes the negative variation of this trope, but the positive version is definitely in use.

Another technique that Schopenhauer writes about is to ask lots of questions of the person that you are arguing with which will confuse the target and make them unsure of what you are actually trying to find out (2013). They will, then, not be sure what—if anything—they should hide, and may also make mistakes that you can use against them. Along with this and other techniques, Schopenhauer also suggests that you make your opponent angry, no matter what, because "when he is angry he is incapable of judging aright, and perceiving where his advantage lies. You can make him angry by doing him repeated injustice, or practicing some kind of chicanery, and being generally insolent" (2013, p. 8). This is probably the rule that is most followed by trolls, and is the procedure that is most often used as well. It's easiest, but also is the one that requires the most knowledge of the opponent. In another section, he recommends that if you stumble into something that makes the opponent angry, "you must urge it with all the more zeal; not only because it is a good thing to make him angry, but because it may be presumed that you have here put your finger on the weak side of his case, and that just here he is more open to attack than even for the moment you perceive" (2013, p. 13).

One rule that has been followed often, not just when referring to groups, but when referring to acts, is his twelfth:

> If the conversation turns upon some general conception which has no particular name, but requires some figurative or metaphorical designation, you must begin by choosing a metaphor that is favourable to your proposition. For instance, the names used to denote the two political parties in Spain, Serviles and Liberates, are obviously chosen by the latter. The name Protestants is chosen by themselves, and also the name Evangelicals; but the Catholics call them heretics. (Schopenhauer, 2013, p. 9)

Renaming acts and groups is a common technique used to make some groups seem worse than they are and some acts not as bad as they are. This is mostly used for groups and ideas related to gender and race.

Schopenhauer even suggests that you should try to jump to your conclusion if it looks like your opponent is winning, and pretend that you have won instead ("even if it does not follow") (2013, p. 10). If you proclaim triumph you may succeed in doing so even if it doesn't make any sense for you to claim that you won. This technique was used during the 2016 Presidential Election debates. This is not the only procedure that works that probably should not. For example, he suggests that rhetors should use *ad hominem* attacks when possible (XVI). Additionally, should the opponent say something to the effect of being in support of assisted suicide, you should jump to something like, "Why don't you kill yourself then?" Despite this sounding very juvenile, it does work in the case of some online arguments because it may make the opponent disengage (and if the goal is silencing that is a "win").

Instead of calling the arguments of others out as superficial (or "sophistical"), Schopenhauer (2013) suggests that people meet the argument with a counterargument that is just as superficial. In short, you are to show how superficial their argument is by highlighting it with one of your own. This mirrors the way this type of rhetoric interacts with the media—it highlights the ridiculous by imitating the worst parts of it and exploiting it as well. Likewise, Schopenhauer (2013) says that by being contradictory you can make someone exaggerate their statement, which proves how superficial or thin it may be. It drives a person "into extending beyond its proper limits a statement which, at all events within those limits and in itself, is true; and when you refute this exaggerated form of it, you look as though you had also refuted his original statement" (Schopenhauer 2013, p. 12). This is related to the *retorsio argumenti*, in which you turn the argument of your opponent against him or herself.

Schopenhauer (2013) also recommends such procedures as creating a diversion such as talking about something else—but I would also add that memes are a wonderful way to create such a diversion. They can be used to make fun of an opponent, sure, and often are, but image macros especially have the ability to distract not only the opponent but the audience. Schopenhauer's suggestion is that the diversion be brought in to attack the opponent as well—but a simple distraction might be enough to sway the argument in your favor if you suspect you are losing.

Lastly, Schopenhauer (2013) suggests that the rhetor become "personal, insulting, rude, as soon as you perceive that your opponent has the upper hand, and that you are going to come off worst" (p. 21). This suggests that when trolls are rudest is when they think they are losing. This quite honestly works—as a piece of procedural rhetoric, fighting back the most when you are losing seems obvious. However, if the person you are arguing with suddenly makes the argument personal, it probably means they are losing on a different rhetorical front. Remaining calm and logical as *they* become emotional can lead to a win. As Schopenhauer (2013) explains, " . . . in becoming personal you leave the subject altogether, and turn your attack to his person, by remarks of an offensive and spiteful character. It is an appeal from the virtues of the intellect to the virtues of the body, or to mere animalism. This is a very popular trick, because everyone is able to carry it into effect; and so it is of frequent application" (p. 22).

And so, the way of the troll in using procedural rhetoric is explained (and really is nothing new). Schopenhauer's techniques can also be applied to media and politics, as well as the rhetoric employed by hate websites.

These techniques are augmented by the ad-hoc and enhanced when they are used by many anonymous rhetors at once. Anonymity is one of the strongest techniques available online, and deserves further analysis here.

Anonymity as Rhetorical Device

I have briefly discussed before that by taking on a group moniker (in this case, Anonymous) that the ad-hoc has become not only powerful but very unique in their ability to act online and in real life. This is partly because the power of the word *anonymous* already carried—it was in many online spaces, automatically given to anyone who did not name themselves. This meant that when Anonymous began, lots of people were being assigned a name that meant they were members of a group (and could, perhaps, speak for the group) that did not even realize that they had gained membership.

Anonymity is its own sort of rhetorical device. In eliminating personal ethos for group ethos, any person can take on the ethos of the group. As Anonymous has shifted from a group known for attacking random people who anger its members to going after religions, world governments, and sometimes even other ad-hocs like GamerGate, that group identity has shifted from a negative one to a positive one—if not still a terrifying one.

When ad-hoc replaces personal ethos, and when anyone can join the ad-hoc, that significantly shifts the rhetorical triangle. Is the speaker more or less important when the speaker is a group? When the speaker speaks with one thousand voices, is ethos gained or diminished?

One way to examine this issue is to look at identity in games and see how those identities might affect procedural rhetoric. In James Paul Gee's *What Video Games Have to Teach us about Learning and Literacy* (2003), Gee writes that there are three identities in video games: virtual, real, and projective. In games, he says, there is first the virtual identity which is the singular identity of the character that you play in the virtual world (his is the elf "Bead-bead"). In systems where you name yourself something, this is your pseudonym. In games, it is often an avatar.

In the Game of the Internet, this bears resemblance to the situation when many different people might play a single character at once. When you play a Mario game, for example, all players play as Mario (except those weird people who choose to play as Luigi and awesome people who prefer Yoshi). Even when videos are posted online that say who is playing, it is still just *Mario* up there on the screen. When people post *as* Anonymous, representing all Anons, they take on the same sort of identity. Everyone who picks up the Game of the Internet plays as Anonymous. They take on that virtual identity.

But much like playing as Mario, many of these people don't actually see themselves as becoming their virtual identity on the screen. When Phillips (2015) interviews trolls, she describes many of them as having a "mask of trolling," which is the virtual identity that they take on in order to be a troll. They might not believe, personally, in what they are saying any more than they might believe in their need to rescue the Princess (Daisy *or* Peach) in a Mario game. It's just a thing that they do. This is also a little like watching a group of people (hundreds, in the case of *Twitch Plays Pokémon*) control a single game with a single set of controls—it can be a little chaotic, but eventually a sort of order rises out of the chaos.

Gee (2003) goes on to describe another identity, the *projective* identity. The projective identity

> play[s] on two senses of the word "project," meaning both "to project one's values and desires onto the virtual character" (Bead-bead, in this case) and "seeing the virtual character as one's own project in the making, a creature whom I imbue with a certain trajectory though time defined by my aspirations for what I want that character to be and become (within the limitations of her capacities, of course)." (p. 55)

The projective identity can be used, in part, to explain the shift that has happened in Anonymous (while 4Chan has largely stagnated and sprouted other ad-hocs meant for more specific purposes). Since Anonymous was actually trying to do things—even if those first things were things like shutting up a feminist like BB—there were many hands steering a single entity. Much like a giant Ouija board, slowly the hive mind of Anonymous was created, and it wasn't interested in just trolling the people that 4Chan had always trolled. Instead, this projective identity included peoples' own interests. They wanted to protest groups like Scientology that made them angry, and they wanted to fight ISIS, and they wanted to take a stand for net neutrality—in short, the projective identity is what makes Anonymous into the group that it is today.

The third identity is the most basic—the real-world identity. This identity doesn't often enter into the Game of the Internet from the side of the trolls and procedures, except that there usually is a person behind the things that you read on your screen. However, that person might not have anything to do with the rhetoric that you see represented there. At its most basic, that person might be going to an IRC channel and copying and pasting (sorry—copypasta-ing) text to use to harass you. They might be following procedures that other trolls have taught them. They might be posting memes because they understand that is part of the game. They might be doing a lot of things, but what they are doing is using the tools available to them to play as a virtual identity in a virtual world.

So what sort of ethos does that build?

For one, the virtual identity is the most important to Anonymous's ethos. It is the only one that every group member can take on. As individuals are not meant to use this ad-hoc as their "personal army," most people who try to insert their real-world identity into the world of Anonymous will find that it doesn't work well or they become targets themselves (as is true for the woman who attempted to start Back-Trace Security).

But the projective identity obviously has a lot of power too. If enough of the members of an ad-hoc all want a change, that change will happen. When Kevin Kelley writes about how "more is different," he writes about how schools of fish and flocks of birds all change directions at once. It looks effortless, but requires group cohesion. That is true of Anonymous as well, if the projective identities of the players all want the group to change, it probably will.

Anonymous's ethos is also determined a lot by the media, but they are experts at influencing the media. Ad-Hocs that want to use the media to build their ethos or spread their message must become just as adept at using the media to their own ends.

Alexander Haslam and Stephen Reicher (2012) argue, in a study of conformity and the Milgram experiment, that anonymity might not have as much of an effect on the outcome of whether a group is destructive or constructive than one might assume. The original Milgram experiment made the claim that anonymity leads to awful behavior. However, Haslam and Reicher (2012) say that group dynamics exist more. "If the norm of the group is to be destructive, well actually then anonymity can enhance that . . . But if the norm of the group is to be constructive, then anonymity can enhance that" (as quoted in Phillips, 2015, p. 156). If this type of rhetoric (trolling/procedural) is only destructive I also do not believe that we would see the people who participate able to bring about creation in the way that they do either. They want their projective identities to be creative, even if they never have the chance to claim "I made that" when looking at various memes online.

Trolls celebrate and insist upon their group identity. Being anonymous means being able to be an asshole, sure, but it also allows someone to play with creation without having to worry about someone telling you that you are an awful artist or aren't funny. If something you say doesn't work it isn't tied to your name, and it is easy to start over. Anonymity gives people the capability of starting over again and again and again, and they can choose to only take credit when they meet with a success. There is a reason that anonymity and these groups are often associated with failing—it is because, quite honestly, that they see failing as funny, as a natural extension of what normally happens online, and as something to be shared instead of hidden. Anonymity also allows the real-world identities involved to take on multiple other identities, as we do in games, and see how they feel, see what people might say to them, and to play out real-world conversations as them. Certainly not all of those identities are healthy and many are downright aggressive, but they are still *virtual* in every sense for many of the people that are posting as them.

For those mostly interested in preventing trolling or the Game of the Internet from happening in their own spaces, the easiest way to do it is to prevent real-world identities from being shared in that space. Many communities on Reddit will delete any post that shares a real-world identity for that reason. It is not dangerous just for your job (who might find you and criticize something you have to say or declare you as being unprofessional), but it is also dangerous because it attracts trolls.

People playing the Game of the Internet and using procedural rhetoric on it very well might think that everyone should be playing. This is *fun*, they say, *everyone should be like us*. Of course, not everyone is going to jump on the troll train. However, there is something a bit addictive about the style of humor that is contained within this game. Nothing is serious? Anything can be made fun of? Surely most of us have found a place and time in our daily work lives where we would love to poke fun at a meeting or an administrator. Trolls see themselves as teachers in this form of rhetoric and interaction (Phillips, 2015). They expect everyone else to eventually have to catch up. They are teachers, and they see great pedagogues who came before them as their ancestors.

SOCRATES: THE FIRST TROLL?

One of the most fun Internet searches you can run if you happen to be a rhetoric teacher is "Was Socrates a Troll?" In short, trolls argue that Socrates was one of them—some of the methods he used to teach align nicely with Schopenhauer, and they study him as a way to learn how to argue and troll better.

Yes, people are studying Socrates (Plato's version) as a way to learn how to be better jerks on the Internet. If you are surprised, consider that Socrates loves to trick people into agreeing with him, and so do trolls. As an introduction to the way he is venerated, this is his current Encyclopedia Dramatica entry:

> Socrates was a famous IRL troll of pre-internets Greece credited with inventing the first recorded trolling technique and otherwise laying the foundation of the science of lulz. He is widely considered to be the most irritating man in history. Accounts of his successful trolls are in the form of tl;dr copypasta on Plato's LiveJournal. There they have been pwning NORPS for thousands of years in Philosophy 101 classes around the world. Socrates was v& and b& IRL in 399BC for grievous trolling. (Encyclopedia Dramatica, 2015)

Having then briefly quoted the man himself, the entry goes on to state:

For fun, he lured pretentious moralfags called sophists (ancient Greece's equivalent of wikipaedos) into pointless drama by stroking their egos with obviously ironic compliments. After lolling them into a false state of security, he employed the famous Socratic Method of Trolling which consists of the following steps:

1. Ask a bunch of questions about shit nobody cares about
2. Be blatantly condescending while pretending to agree
3. Raep your victim with logic
4. Pretend to be objective and ignorant
5. Put forth a batshit insane position for lulz
6. ???
7. Profit

This method earned Socrates many flawless victories but also made him many enemies like Aristophanes, a furfag with a thing for frogs, who wrote a play in which a lizzard shits on Socrates's head. After the invention of the internet, The Socratic Method was refined by chantards and EDiots into The Comprehensive Theory of Lulz. (Encyclopedia Dramatica, 2015)

While perhaps not the words I would expect them to use, I would love if my college freshmen had such an understanding of the Socratic method. (The "???" from the list is a reference to a *South Park* episode about underwear gnomes that steal underwear, have no idea what to do with it, and expect to make a profit anyway) (Parker, 1998).

Elsewhere on the Web, people on Quora argue that they don't believe Socrates was a troll because he was after capital-T Truth, and trolls simply are in it for the lulz (Engel, 2012). While that might be true in some instances, it could also be argued that trolls that are involved in Anonymous do want to find the Truth as do those who are involved in ad-hocs like Reddit. When the Boston Marathon Bombing occurred, members of Reddit attempted to use their numbers to find the person responsible. Unfortunately, they accused the wrong person—but they were invested in finding the truth. Wikileaks, as well, is ultimately concerned with sharing Truth with the entire world, no matter the consequences of that Truth.

Weev, the hacker discussed in an earlier chapter, states that Socrates would have been a troll if trolls existed (Phillips, 2015). Socrates attempted to be confrontational, he wanted to provoke a reaction, and he wanted to undermine the establishment so badly that he ended up being put to death for it. Socrates' method of teaching pursued answers in the same ways that trolls often do, even though they take that "approach to its most antagonistic conclusions" (Phillips, 2015, p. 127).

If studying trolling means that people also study Socrates, I'd have to give at least some trolling behaviors a pass. Yet, I've not run into a single freshman that thinks Socrates is awesome, so either I don't have many students who are trolls or—if I do—they are simply learning the behaviors from one another instead of studying from the source.

> . . . the fact that trolls have chosen as their intellectual mascot one of the most venerated and fetishized figures in the Western tradition, whose rhetorical method is taught to every college undergraduate in the United States, is significant in itself. Also of significance is the fact that, while trolls and trolling behaviors are condemned as aberrational, similarly antagonistic—and highly gendered—rhetorical methods are presumed to be something to which every eighteen-year-old should aspire. This is, to say the very least, a curious double standard. Trolling might be more conspicuously outrageous, offensive, and damaging than traditional discursive modes, but what does it say about the cloth if misogyny can so easily be cut from it? (Phillips, 2015, p. 128)

TROLLING IS JUST COOKERY: GORGIAS AND PROCEDURALISM

In the *Gorgias*, Plato uses Socrates to attack rhetoric as being something akin to "mere cookery"—something that anyone can learn and master, no matter whether he or she knows anything about the subject being discussed at all. This is *exactly* the way that trolls proceduralize and game rhetoric online. Anyone can play their game if they get into the right IRC channel, pick up an Anonymous identity, and start posting the right things. Of course, even trolls have a learning curve—"newbs" are going to get made fun of and have to pick up the language quickly or else they will not make it as part of the ad-hoc. However, that does not change the fact that they have turned persuasion online into a thing that can be copied, pasted, and learned very quickly by just about anyone—even the very young boys living in their parents' house that a lot of people assume trolls are.

In the *Gorgias*, Socrates argues that rhetoric is not really an art in the same way that painting is an art. Instead, it is more like cooking—something that can be learned by recipe. They are trying to answer what rhetoric is. In the dialogue, you can see that Socrates actually does use some of the techniques that Schopenhauer discusses. For example, when Polus asks what is rhetoric, Socrates rephrases it into a completely different question so that he can go on a tangent and argue whether rhetoric is an art, and ignores the question of what rhetoric is to begin with:

> Pol. I will ask; and do you answer me, Socrates, the same question which Gorgias, as you suppose, is unable to answer: What is rhetoric?
>
> Soc. Do you mean what sort of an art?
>
> Pol. Yes.
>
> Soc. To say the truth, Polus, it is not an art at all, in my opinion.
>
> Pol. Then what, in your opinion, is rhetoric? (Plato, 380 BCE)

He goes on to say that rhetoric is, instead, to perhaps be a sort of experience in "producing a sort of delight and gratification." Polus argues that if this is true, then rhetoric must be a fine thing, but naturally Socrates disagrees (because Socrates always disagrees). He changes the question back to what rhetoric is yet again:

> Soc. What are you saying, Polus? Why do you ask me whether rhetoric is a fine thing or not, when I have not as yet told you what rhetoric is?
>
> Pol. Did I not hear you say that rhetoric was a sort of experience?
>
> Soc. Will you, who are so desirous to gratify others, afford a slight gratification to me?
>
> Pol. I will. (Plato, 380 BCE)

Socrates, at all times, has complete control over the conversation and later even tells Polus what to do:

> Soc. Will you ask me, what sort of an art is cookery?

> Pol. What sort of an art is cookery?
>
> Soc. Not an art at all, Polus.
>
> Pol. What then?
>
> Soc. I should say an experience.
>
> Pol. In what? I wish that you would explain to me.
>
> Soc. An experience in producing a sort of delight and gratification, Polus.
>
> Pol. Then are cookery and rhetoric the same?
>
> Soc. No, they are only different parts of the same profession. (Plato, 380 BCE)

At this point, Socrates renames what rhetoric is by equating it with cookery—another suggestion that is made by Schopenhauer.

Socrates drags a question out of Polus at this point, so that he may answer what type of profession he is speaking of when he defines both rhetoric and cookery:

> Soc. In my opinion then, Gorgias, the whole of which rhetoric is a part is not an art at all, but the habit of a bold and ready wit, which knows how to manage mankind: this habit I sum up under the word "flattery"; and it appears to me to have many other parts, one of which is cookery, which may seem to be an art, but, as I maintain, is only an experience or routine and not an art:-another part is rhetoric, and the art of attiring and sophistry are two others: thus there are four branches, and four different things answering to them. And Polus may ask, if he likes, for he has not as yet been informed, what part of flattery is rhetoric: he did not see that I had not yet answered him when he proceeded to ask a further question: Whether I do not think rhetoric a fine thing? But I shall not tell him whether rhetoric is a fine thing or not, until I have first answered, "What is rhetoric?" For that would not be right, Polus; but I shall be happy to answer, if you will ask me, What part of flattery is rhetoric?
>
> Pol. I will ask and do you answer? What part of flattery is rhetoric?

Soc. Will you understand my answer? Rhetoric, according to my view, is the ghost or counterfeit of a part of politics.

Pol. And noble or ignoble?

Soc. Ignoble, I should say, if I am compelled to answer, for I call what is bad ignoble: though I doubt whether you understand what I was saying before.

Gor. Indeed, Socrates, I cannot say that I understand myself.

Soc. I do not wonder, Gorgias; for I have not as yet explained myself, and our friend Polus, colt by name and colt by nature, is apt to run away.

Gor. Never mind him, but explain to me what you mean by saying that rhetoric is the counterfeit of a part of politics. (Plato, 380 BCE)

Rhetoric is not an art of the truth, but is instead the art of telling people what they want to hear (certainly true online—or telling them the exact opposite of what they want to hear) and he also states that rhetoricians are not virtuous. They are ignoble instead.

Sophists seek to sway public opinion, do so by whatever means necessary, and can give speeches on any topic. Rhetoricians should, instead, seek to find the Truth. Sophists are like cooks to Socrates (and therefore Plato) as he argues that the soul and body are separate and have different arts corresponding to each. Furthermore, it is possible to imitate good or noble arts for both the body and the soul. These simulations do not care what is actually good for body or soul, but instead rely upon flattery to make the connection to body or soul a positive one. Thus, cookery and sophistry both produce experiences, but do so to produce pleasure without considering what is "best." Cookery, to Socrates, could seem to be like medicine. You could potentially give a man who is ailing good food or good medicine and ask which he enjoyed the most. He would most likely (and naturally, even today) pick the good food. However, it is the medicine he needs. It is so with rhetoric versus sophistry. Given both, man will favor what is flattering him and making him feel better about himself even if what he needs to hear (for his Soul) is something else entirely. Despite trolls talking about how they "know how to rhetoric," it seems likely that Socrates would call what they do, by following procedures, sophistry instead.

It might take a great deal more time and space to argue that trolls are sophists and not rhetoricians, but it does seem that procedural rhetoric and sophistry have a great deal in common.

Sophistry, it seems, accepts the idea that anyone can learn to be persuasive, and might embrace the idea that such persuasion can be taught and can be reduced to a pattern that can be followed. However, as much of traditional sophistry has been lost (and procedural rhetoric, such as it is, exists today), comparing this type of rhetoric—or sophistry—to that of machines and/or games makes nearly as much sense. Of course, that is not the only way that we can explain trolling and procedural rhetorics.

CONCLUSION

It might be tempting to say that we should strive to create spaces that are free of trolls while letting trolls have their own spaces to play on like 4Chan. However, the sort of surveillance that is needed to create that sort of safe space (heavy moderation) means that creativity and fun is also foreshortened, if only because users feel afraid of saying the wrong thing. I, myself, have had more posts deleted from the AskWomen subreddit than I care to admit. I don't wish to censor my students that much, let alone strangers on the Internet. Without being given space to play, we don't have a lot of space to learn. While seemingly alien, the procedural rhetorics developed by trolls are connected to the past through some of the most famous rhetors—while digital is different, while more is different, while networked systems are different, this is not an entirely new form of persuasion and it should not be dismissed as not rhetorical.

It is in our nature to determine whether something is good or bad, to be able to determine whether we should be doing one practice or another. We want to do something that matters, something that is approved of by others. And so, agency is most often described as really meaning something wherein a person does something that changes their own life, gives them more freedom, or gives that freedom to others (Nealon, 2007). When you follow the rules, when you play the game, can what you are doing ever really be considered agency? If you are part of a swarm, do you have agency or does the swarm?

To have agency, you don't have to break all the rules, you just have to have power over the outcome of the game. You need to be able to negotiate the consequences. That might happen by being able to define your own winning conditions, or it might be by learning to take control over procedural rhetorics yourself, or it might even happen by learning how to. In the final chapter, I look at the way that procedural rhetorics, gaming, and even trolling can be built in the framework of otherwise completely ordinary writing classes.

6 The Pedagogy of Play

In this chapter I tie the previous information into composition pedagogy. How can the lessons learned by looking at Internet communities and conversations as games be brought into the composition classroom? Should they? I present several assignments that expand upon gaming in composition pedagogy to not only present a rhetoric of play, but to also take advantage of procedural rhetoric and teach students how to use procedural rhetoric in digital writing. I also will discuss how analyzing these conversations as procedurally rhetorical and how analyzing fallacies using Schopenhauer (2013) can empower students to understand rhetoric currently used in digital and political context. These assignments were used in 2013–2015 sections of Technical Writing and Applied Digital Writing at Frostburg State University with results reported in the chapter. I will also discuss possibilities for creating online communities for MOOC courses that could engage students through procedural rhetorics into this state—which most of our current activities via message boards, wikis, and blogs for students simply do not.

I believe that the rhetorical climate of 2017 is one that does not lend itself easily to classical rhetoric. We have politicians who use insults and anger in many of the ways that Schopenhauer (2013) wrote about. Living online means that most people will experience harassment and hate at some point in their lives. Between needing to make sense of media manipulation of facts, politics themselves, and their own digital experiences, students need to learn about more than classical rhetoric to become engaged citizens in today's world.

However, assignments should not put students at undue risk, nor should they ask students to become trolls of the hateful sort. No one should encourage their students to use swatting or doxxing, of course, but they also should discuss more liberal techniques such as doc dumping critically to examine how much they value free speech versus the potential for disrupting peace. As a result, assignments and courses that take these types of rhetoric into account must be carefully crafted to teach such rhetorical practices in an embedded manner, and one that is unlikely to open students to harm.

More generally, as an instructor of rhetoric and composition, I first took this project on as a way of determining two things: (1) Why some very well-crafted arguments by online feminists were doomed to failure and (2) how I could teach my students to not have their own arguments result in such a failure. When I was a grad student, I had been repeatedly asked to blog, to digitally publish, and to make my work "real" for myself in whatever way possible. As an instructor, I am quick to want the same things for my students—I don't want the projects that we create in the classroom that are truly innovative and interesting to stall in the classroom and never be seen by the outside world. That, to me, does not seem to be a successful use of the technology that we have been afforded.

However, no matter how I framed the assignments that I had once been given, I was ultimately met with the same sorts of resistance that I had once given my instructors by my own students. They did not want to blog about serious topics, no matter how interesting the subjects were to them during the relatively safe classroom discussions that we would have. They would write brilliant papers, but only parts of their best arguments would make it onto their websites (or, better yet, they would just copy and paste the whole thing, probably never to be read again unless somebody plagiarized it). Other websites were turned in with two lines of text. The rhetorical techniques that were so useful to them in the classroom were failing in online spaces, and part of my impetus in studying what works (no matter how ribald and crude) has been to begin to understand why that is.

Although much further study is needed to support the claims that I make about gaming and classroom practice, I do believe that procedural rhetoric and gaming rhetorics have a place in composition classrooms. Assignments created from a place of play, gaming and using technology to learn rather than as finished products work pretty well. Building an ad-hocracy in a classroom is difficult, but not impossible. Even a simple admission on the part of the instructor about how common rhetorical techniques often don't carry over to digital systems will help to build classrooms and assignments that can ultimately lead students to know how to navigate the tricky rhetorical territory of online spaces and create the sorts of good discussions we want to see.

I was once asked if I really wanted my students to be creating things like Derpy Hooves. He said it like it was a bad thing. "Derpy" is a character on *My Little Pony: Friendship is Magic* (2010–2017). The show became a viral sensation, as I noted earlier in the book, after an article was published condemning it as just a way to sell toys. 4Chan said that simply wasn't the case, started watching, and within days spawned hundreds of memes. These were eventually taken to their own board (PonyChan) and a huge fandom was born. There are still a lot of male, college-aged *My Little Pony* fans. Quite simply—yes. If my students created a viral media sensation that affected the source media, I'd be pretty excited. Despite the negative Web presence of 4Chan, the producers of *MLP: FiM* not only were able to see the good in the site, but realize that their fan input could ultimately be used to increase viewership and sales. This is the sort of action that I wish my classrooms could take—even if they did not directly influence a television show, there is no reason to presume they could not directly affect someone outside of their classmates.

To answer the question much the way I did then—I would be thrilled if my students created a viral phenomenon that eventually was featured on a television show. I don't care if you can call it "trolling." The sort of work that was done in highlighting Derpy in the background of an episode of *My Little Pony*, then giving her a story and a personality that the show's creators eventually used, is amazing work. I'm not even sure if I would know how much extra credit to give a student project that pulled off the seemingly impossible. So yes, I do think that creating viral media takes rhetorical action, and I do think that that is something my students should be doing in class. The problem is that I cannot simply say, "Today we are going to create viral memes everybody!" It wouldn't work. These types of memes are created by completely different circumstances than a forced group activity in a composition class. One potential way to game the system, though, would be to get the class an audience outside of class itself and have them interact with them.

GETTING OUR STUDENTS AN AUDIENCE ONLINE

There are two ways to get noticed online: either you play the game, or you definitely don't play the game. People in the middle—those people who aren't doing anything explicitly against the rules—are not going to get noticed. We have two choices in getting our students noticed in digital publication—procedural scholarship and classical scholarship.

Traditionally, we've leaned towards classical (non-procedural) scholarship, aka Traditional Rhetoric that is then shared digitally. Professors and Directors of Composition face the same demands they always have—people in other departments and corporate interests that claim our students cannot write, leading us to creating essay assignments that are formal and enforce the rules of academic writing. The problem today with digital classical scholarship is that the instructor is having students write about the same old stuff—abortion, feminism, racism, global warming, obesity, or whatever your students show interest in—and put it online, instead of developing new types of writing that are better shared with digital systems. Students might write a paper and develop it into a website, post to a blog, or even make a video—but they are *usually* judged on their engagement with traditional rhetoric and traditional academic writing. Even the best multimedia projects about these ideas are likely to get a single viewing and then be pushed aside—because we've seen it before but also because it isn't very innately interesting. It doesn't really do anything you couldn't do on paper, and it certainly doesn't encourage you to show your friends (again, there are probably exceptions to the rule, but most student projects on these topics aren't those exceptions). If they do get outside notice, they may get comments in the style that 4Chan and Anonymous leave, telling them that the Internet shouldn't be serious business, that they are doing it wrong, or that they, themselves, are simply wrong in their opinions. None of these are things that I would want to see happen to my students online.

On the other hand, if you were a completely different instructor who happened to be invested in enforcing the rules of traditional rhetoric, that website or YouTube video might be of interest purely because it does break so many of the Rules of the Internet. It attempts to use the Internet seriously, and in doing so fails to recognize that nobody really cares about such serious usage during their own free time (or as Shirky would put it—their own cognitive surplus time). You have to be *really* good—a really good writer, a really good filmmaker, a really good designer— to make this sort of site work. Even then, you might find yourself a target for groups like 4Chan and Anonymous as well as all those who are well aware of their techniques. YouTube comments represent the scourge of the earth—when students do share videos with YouTube, unless they are funny ones I encourage them to turn off the comments. While we all occasionally have a student or group of students who are just that capable of making something outstanding on a serious topic, we all also know that those students are relatively rare. Many are simply in development—getting there, but still several years from creating amazing media.

Regardless, if we care about digital systems, we ask our students to write these things, we ask our students to do these things, and a certain percentage of them are going to be flamed and harassed for it. I, myself, was harassed for posting on my blog for a Feminisms and Rhetorics course during PhD studies about men's rights activists. I actually was speaking about one, in particular, and someone who I considered a friend. But a group found the link and hundreds of comments later I was beginning to wonder how I was ever going to get a grade for this material.

If we have our students post, are they likely to end up as a target for Anonymous? It's highly unlikely. They certainly could fight back hard enough and long enough (and we teach them to do this when we talk about civic discourse and not allowing racism and sexism to exist in a safe space like our classrooms), but at this point I do not believe that any enemies listed with Anonymous have come from a school project. Since many of the members of Anonymous and 4Chan are young (college-aged and high school-aged students), they may even recognize that sometimes teachers make you make things you'd never do on your own, and that these things aren't worth targeting.

But procedural scholarship could very well produce something other than a wiki or a blog or a website that is rarely, if ever, viewed outside of the classroom. Procedural scholarship has this potential because it is funny, quirky, and witty in a way that traditional projects often aren't. Best of all, this sort of online publishing is the kind that you might just show your friends, who might show their friends. It's the type that might get views from random YouTube searches. It's the kind that is more likely, at this historical date, to get students an audience outside of the classroom and if that is one of the true aims of the instructor then assignments and projects should be designed in a way that follow at least some of the Rules of the Internet.

Making your classroom into a space that allows play and gaming is not about teaching with games every day (though there are some games, such as the board game *Argue!* and *Apples to Apples* that I use nearly every term), but is instead about taking what is different about games from the other forms of media, rhetorics, and pedagogies that we are used to and making use of that difference (Wark, 2007). McKenzie Wark writes that a gamer theory should be about thinking about what games say about the changes in our social and technical relations with one another—adding them and their logic to writing theory and pedagogy is just one step to rethinking the role of technology in our writing classrooms.

Play is difficult to define, but it does have a place in our history and our classrooms. Wark writes that "To approach it, to think this unthinkable category of play, is to play in and against language. Gamer theory calls for concepts that make the now rather familiar world of the digital game strange again" (2007, p. 225).

We say that we want our students to be cyborgs, to be flexible, to be able to adapt to new and changing technologies, to make these technologies a part of their lives, and to be able to use them to their advantage in the writing and argumentative communications. But why do we not want them to be players as well?

Jesper Juul (2005) believes that it is very important for students to begin to learn how to be procedurally literate—to not just be able to read and write and use computers, to be able to "read and write processes, to engage procedural representation and aesthetics, to understand the interplay between the culturally-embedded practice of human meaning-making and technically-mediated processes" (p. 245). In many cases, our society has interpreted this call to learn process as a call to learn code. Toys that teach coding to toddlers exist such as Fisher-Price's Think & Learn caterpillar toy, and lots of people sign up for Codeacademy. Video games can teach these things, if used "properly," as they ask the player to interact with models of processes, teach "biased perspectives" of the way things work, and ask us to directly engage and criticize them as we play (p. 245). But they are not, in any way, the only such processes that would help students to develop a critical engagement with procedural literacy. Part of what I will do here, then, is to start thinking of assignments that teach processes without saying "this is a process, please create a new one."

Video games may not be the best way to teach procedural literacy in writing classrooms at all. Perhaps one reason is that games that are designed by game creators (like the ones we play on our computers and video game consoles) do not allow the user as many options as we would like (yet). There is a right way and a wrong way to play most games (with notable exceptions like *World of Warcraft* where players can complete quests or not, join guilds or not, and advance or not, or *LittleBigPlanet* that allows players to create their own levels). As Ian Bogost writes, "Procedural representations do not necessarily support user interaction. Many computational simulation methods make claims about processes in the material world, but limit user participation significantly" (Bogost, 2006, p. 40). But the Game of the Internet is wide open—with the only controls coming from the dominant ad-hocs, and perhaps the Game of the Classroom is best modeled after these than after video games and their ilk.

Clay Shirky (2005) says that we should not ask why people do things for free such as edit Wikipedia, and instead should ask why they do them at all if we hope to encourage students to submit labor to online creation and causes. I think that when we ask our students to participate in things like online discussion, blogging, fandom, and gaming we have to think of the real reasons that they might use these outside of the classroom as well. Why do people participate in online discussion? I venture that a lot of people just don't understand why anybody would want to do this. Many of these people are fellow teachers and our students. We assign on-line discussion questions—they go relatively unanswered. What we have to understand is why anybody participates in online discussion at all, in addition to what can be learned and gained from it. How do we set up a situation in which people might actually *want* to discuss something, rather than feeling forced? One such situation is, of course, a game. An-other might be an assignment that uses gaming rhetoric or immersion without being a game itself.

We should avoid situations where students *feel* that they are digital sharecropping (doing online work for free, as Shirky defines it)—especially since most of them pay for the privilege to be in our classes. Some of them would undoubtedly view editing Wikipedia as work—after all, it is! That is why the idea of gaming and play within the writing system is so important—if we use the Internet in the same way that the best users of it do, students will recognize that we're not farming them out as digital sharecroppers.

4Chan's memes, and hopefully their creativity, could be harnessed for classroom assignments. Because lolcats are an easy example of a mash-up, and because tools exist online to create them without a digital camera or even photo editor (something that their original creators bemoan, as you used to have to know a little about editing software to make them), they are an easy entry-level assignment into digital rhetoric, especially if thinking about the rhetoric of humor. Any student, no matter their level of comfort with a computer, can create one of these. Furthermore, because the best lolcats, theorists, or any other photo one wishes to lol-isize play off cultural stereotypes and common cultural literacies, they can also be a way for students to create rhetorically complex messages in a necessarily small space. They are just one procedure to articulate an argument within a swarm that can be used by the digital population at large.

Memes are also a way to build community. Mike Hubler and Diane Bell studied how a mailing list (and the things that take place on it) can be used to create community (they call it "world building") (2001). What worked best, at times, for that world building as a certain kind of laughter and shared in-jokes—not always the behavior that we want to cherish in our writing center staff, but from personal experience I can say that it is sometimes useful to vent. "As the community establishes the outline of its own borders, Hubler and Bell argue, a set of shared experiences and expectations emerges; the resulting content feeds into and sustains an interconnected nest of constitutive content, which simultaneously contextualizes and reconfigures the explicit meaning(s) of additional content" (Phillips, 2015, pp. 30–31). In other words, groups form memes, and those memes help them to create communities. We need to be able to create memes to build better communities.

ASSIGNMENTS CREATED FROM A PERSPECTIVE OF PLAY

The assignments in this section have been developed to fulfill different needs for different student populations, and they also experiment with different parts of play and procedural rhetoric. For each I will include an assignment description and assignment sheet (except for the MOOC and Alternate Reality Class) and a discussion.

The Game Study Project (ENGL3010, ENG438, IDIS150, Wayne State University, Baker College, Frostburg State University)

One of my favorite long-standing projects in class is the "Game Study." This paper is situated in classes that are reading part or all of Gee's *What Video Games Have to Teach Us About Learning and Literacy* (2004). I have now done this project as part of a junior-level writing course, in a senior-level writing course for English majors, and also a freshman-level interdisciplinary course about video games. It introduces students to conducting ethnographic research.

For the project, students are asked to choose a game (video or board game, though video games are easier to tie to the text) and play through at least an hour or two of gameplay. They then have to ask a friend or another member of the class to participate in their study. We talk about sample sizes (most notably that a sample size of one or two is not enough for firm conclusions), IRB paperwork, how to write non-leading questions, and how to do ethical human research and not interfere in the process of the people playing, and they are sent off to do a very brief, small study of how someone might learn how to play a game. Students take ethnographic field notes and write up a small paper that proposes a hypothesis that could be proven by a longer, larger study and report their results to the course.

Students *sometimes* (in upper level courses) realize that I am immersing them in the semiotic domain of being a games researcher. Even if they don't, part of the debrief of the assignment is telling them that that is what they just experienced. Whether they realize this trickery or not, most enjoy the process of getting to "create knowledge" rather than just read about it in a book, as they have done up until that point.

Students have also reported some interesting results. My favorites are the student who had gotten VTech games for her daughter but never allowed her to play and decided to let her play for the project—only to watch her daughter finally master a math concept that she had been struggling with—and the student who thought that she and her sister would "kick her grandma's ass" at the board game Balderdash—only for grandma to win every single game. Students are surprisingly happy to have their initial hypothesis proven wrong, and the best projects do not simply relate to Gee passively but instead actively create new ideas about how we can learn from games.

Game Study Assignment Sheet

This project is connected to your reading of James Paul Gee's *What Video Games Have to Teach Us About Learning and Literacy.* For this project, you will be playing as much of a chosen video game and/or board game as you can given the time frame of the essay. At the very least, you should work through the first few opening missions of most games or play a few times through a board game in order to explore and understand how the game wants you to learn everything necessary to play. How much you choose to play is up to you, but if you pick a game you like hopefully you'll play quite a bit and have a lot to write about! If you have played the game before, I ask that you refresh your memory of the game by playing it again from the beginning, this will help you formulate questions for the next part of the project and remember what the opening of the game and training sections are like if the game has them.

Once you have played your game and we have read through a lot of the book in class, begin to make connections between the concepts that Gee writes about and what you have experienced in game play. Specifically note when the game asks you to learn in situated contexts, how it connects to the 36 learning principles, what "identities" are in use in the game, and how the game gets you to learn things. Be able to draw connections between the book and your gameplay experience.

Once you have played yourself (again, just enough to have a familiarity with the game), you will be studying one or more other people as they learn to play. Find people who have never played the game before (please ask classmates, family, and friends to be guinea pigs—I AM also available). While they play, consider the various methods we will study in class to study a game or gamer—pick the ones that work best for your situation.

Every paper is hopefully going to be very different. You will be asked to present your papers on the day they are due. Remember to use "all means necessary" to show us what you mean about your particular title (hint: YouTube has great gameplay videos that can probably be used for this). Indeed, screenshots and clips may be inserted into or linked to your essay if you believe they can help you make a point (cite them please!) You should also write at least a brief section of the paper on how the video game itself uses rhetoric to keep you playing beyond those first few puzzles.

Grading rubric:	
Length (5–7 pages, at least)	25 points
Spelling/Grammar/MLA/APA Citations	25 points
Development and Use of Gee and other research	50 points

Most students have found this project to be a good introduction to doing independent research, and are able to come up with theses that go beyond "My game demonstrates Gee's principles." However, some do need to be reminded that they should not simply go through the list of thirty-six learning principles and describe how the game does or does not show each one.

I also set very low minimum page limits for papers in my courses as a rule, while asking students to do more writing than could usually fit into that page limit. These projects often run from 15–20 pages, but since I have used this assignment at many different levels, I have found that that tends to scare freshman and even junior-level students. As a result, I set the page count low but tell them they can go over as far as they would like, and they tend to be very proud of the results. In this way, they write something they thought they could never write without the stress intrinsic to writing to a longer length. This is also true of many of the other assignments that follow.

Creating a Game (ENG3010, ENGL438, IDIS150, Wayne State University, Frostburg State University)

As a follow up to the previous paper, I have students create a game. This has been assigned at Wayne State (in ENGL3010: Intermedia Composition) and at Frostburg State (in ENGL438: Applied Digital Writing and IDIS150: Learning from Video Games). When I first created this assignment, I did not work in a classroom with computers, nor did students often carry their own laptops. They worked in groups to create board games, and I asked them to write a brief statement about how those board games used principles of games (Gee), rhetoric, and good design in order to encourage people to play and to teach them a concept from their major. On the final day of the course, I brought doughnuts and everyone played each other's games. There was a wide variety as well—one student created an interactive tutorial game on a DVD that taught other students to play the drums (and brought his drum kit for that purpose), another group made a board game to teach anatomy, and a third made a PowerPoint Jeopardy game about music. The last day of class was the sort of chaos that I wish every day in class could be (of course, there has to be some build up to get to that pay-off).

When I started working at Frostburg State University I was lucky enough to always teach in computer labs, so I changed this project to one that is meant to be a video game, but can be a board game if students prefer. Some students who are artistically inclined do choose the option to make a game on paper, but many choose one of the game engines available to them. I provide them with a number of suggested game engines, including Twine.

As part of the process, we look at real game scripts and flowcharts, read about how real game designers make storyboards and collect media to put into the games. Students are asked to teach a concept, make an argument, or tell a story. Most English majors choose to tell a story. Some adapt famous literature. Science students like to teach concepts. With the release of *Mario Maker* for the Wii U, several students chose to create Mario levels.

In addition to their script, flowchart, and game, students also turn in a write-up that describes *how* their game does what they say it does (in regards to telling a story, making an argument, etc.) and also how it uses some of the principles that we have studied in class (which varies from class to class). Students who are interested in going into game design get to stretch their wings a bit.

As a note, the hardest part of this assignment is playing the games that are created. I have gotten "stuck" trying to beat particularly hard levels more than once, so while this is "fun" it can also be frustrating. I have had other teachers suggest to me that the student should be providing a video playthrough or other materials to make them easier to grade but, for me, part of the fun is playing the games and finding out what they've hidden for me. They make them hard on purpose. They want to stump me. Dare I say they want to troll me? For those that have succeeded, I am most grateful. It took a lot of work to make something so hard I was stuck on it for a week or more.

Game Project Assignment Sheet

In this project, you will be scripting and creating (use free web-based tools or knowledge from other courses) one level of a video game. This level must tell a story, teach a concept, or make an argument. The level can occur anywhere in your imagined game, but if you want to make one that would occur as part of a bigger game in the middle you should explain the action before the level in your script. What you teach, tell, or argue is completely up to you. You should think about Gee's principles, but also consider what you like to play (even if you don't like video games—what would you like if somebody would make it? I, for one, would love a Yoshi First Person Shooter!)

Grading:	
Flowchart	20 points
Script	40 points
Analysis/Principles	15 points
Game	25 points

Potential game engines: Steam for Education (I have 20 licenses available wherein you can build a Portal 2 level for free)

- Twine
- Minecraft
- Game Salad
- Construct 2
- Mario0
- Splodr
- LittleBigPlanet
- Mario Maker
- Quest: http://www.textadventures.co.uk/quest/ can be used to build free online text based adventure games
- Unity (advanced) http://unity3d.com/create-games/
- ARGs (Alternate Reality Games) via websites, videos, etc.
- NovaShell http://www.rtsoft.com/novashell/

For extra credit, I do allow students to share their games online. However, due to the controversy surrounding Twine games from GamerGate (primarily the questioning of whether or not people who use Twine to develop games are "real" designers), part of the process of teaching this project now is discussing game culture, what it means to be a gamer, and safety online. The students who choose to share their games regardless tend to be the very best designers and digital artists who have taken skills from other courses and adapted them in their games. To get the other students a wider audience, I often nominate great text-based games for the English Colloquium, an honors conference held once a year where students get to share great papers and projects with other students and faculty in the department.

As I noted before, the hardest part about implementing this project, other than knowing enough code to help students when they are stuck, is playing the games. However, there are problems beyond students creating clever projects that are difficult to play. Students will develop games on whatever platform they have, and so if you are a Mac user you may find yourself on campus late at night trying to beat their game that must be played on a PC, for example. I have also purchased several games for the explicit purpose of being able to open their files. I could limit them to things that I own, but I sometimes have let students who really want to learn to develop on a platform do so.

Sweded Videos (ENGL3010, ENG102, ENGL438, Wayne State University, Baker College, Frostburg State University)

Jesper Juul writes that the best games include good communication and strategic planning as part of their play and as an incentive to build community—in short, being a part of the community of the game will make you a better player (2005). If we want people to build community online, we have to make communication and strategic planning a necessity. The same is true in classrooms. If we want the classroom to be a community, which is fairly difficult to do in 10–15 weeks, then we need to do more than hold classroom discussions about readings. We need to play well, communicate well, and plan well together—and a game is a great way to get us doing just that. If a classroom involves a game or a game-like assignment, then we can begin to see community building occurring around the rules, the skills of various players, and the gameplay itself (Juul, 2005).

Many multimedia group projects already in use in classrooms today actually take advantage of this fact. Students work in groups to solve a problem, create a multimedia solution, and play with an idea. However, these projects tend to occur at the end of the term. The process goes something like this: writing assignment 1, 2, and 3, followed by a big multimedia group project based in some way upon previous research or around a student's major. Though in real life that might be the way things go (you can't make a website about something until you've researched it thoroughly, for example), I was and am disappointed with the outcome of these types of projects as an instructor. Students would finally engage with one another and with the course material and make something incredible and then the class would be over. I felt as though the one part of the class everyone enjoyed and that they learned the most from always happened at the end.

One development that I have made in my classrooms based upon my work with games is that I no longer put that big project at the end—or if I do, there is also another one that occurs at the beginning of the term. For example, in teaching Composition 2 at both Wayne State University and Baker College of Allen Park, I created an assignment that would use a big multimedia project to facilitate writing—rather than to show off at the end of the term. I call this "using technology to learn" or "using technology to write," much as we refer to one kind of writing that we do as "using writing to learn."

In my sections of ENG3010 (Intermediate Composition) at Wayne State, I made my first assignment of the term a rhetorical analysis of a movie. I had recently seen the film *Be Kind Rewind* (Gondry, 2008), and in the film Jack Black and Mos Def are left in charge of a video store in a poor neighborhood in New Jersey. When Jack Black accidentally erases all the tapes, the already doomed store (it is to be condemned and torn down for condos) seems to be finished. However, the two begin to re-film shortened versions of the movies that have been lost using all of the things that they have around and available to them (I also use "using all available means for persuasion" as a quickie definition of rhetoric in the class). They do not save the store, but the entire town comes together as a cohesive unit, playing with their favorite movies and creating what they call "sweded" versions of the films. The film argues that playing with movies this way and that producing a sweded movie can create community—much as Juul argues that gaming together can create community.

In my class, after showing the film I tell students they are to work in groups to swede (3–8 minute) versions of the movie their group chooses to analyze. After their filming and editing is done, they are then to individually write a rhetorical analysis of the movie based upon the sweding work that they did.

What has remained amazing to me in the years following when I first assigned this project is that students can and do form a very special sort of classroom community around the project. They all step into roles best suited for them, play to their strengths, and ultimately finish a project that they are proud of. They often upload them to Youtube, share them with family and friends, and from that day on are truly excited to come to class. The sort of engagement and energy that I used to experience at the end of the term is now present from this project on during the course.

As for the papers, the essays that are written after this project are more likely to examine the film from the viewpoint of a producer rather than a consumer of media. In other words, students look at the films as something that somebody made—not just something they happened to watch. One of the main goals I had in beginning this project was to get students to stop simply summarizing the object of their rhetorical analysis for me and to actually get into the stuff that made that object work. Talking about various part of film criticism and terms had not had the effect I wanted in the past.

The sweded films, however, did. My best example occurred during a recent term at Baker College of Allen Park. Students working in one group chose to work with *E.T.* simply because one of them owned the film and another had a stuffed E.T. from when they were a kid. They went through the first week of filming and were discouraged, telling me that it "just didn't look right" and that they "didn't know what was wrong." Honestly, I had no idea either, but suggested that they watch the film again to see what was missing.

It turns out that a quick change in camera angle was all that was needed to fix the project. Most of the original film *E.T.* is purposely filmed at about waist height to your average adult. This forces adults who are watching the movie to look at it from "kid height," so to speak, and forces you to take on the perspective of Elliott, the boy in the movie that befriends E.T. A quick change of their own camera angle made the movie "feel" right *and* gave them all an interesting topic for their rhetorical analysis. As they researched, they discovered that when Steven Spielberg was a young boy his parents divorced, and he created an imaginary friend that was very much like E.T. Connecting this with the forced perspective in the movie created some of the most interesting student papers that I've read in this genre to date.

Students also become part of a larger phenomenon when I ask them to make these sweded movies. Sweding became popular after *Be Kind Rewind's* original 2008 release, as thousands of people went out, sweded their own movies, and put them on YouTube. I do not require students to share their films in this way, but many do. One group who remade *Napoleon Dynamite* even won a $500 prize in an online contest. Other groups may have gotten less fortune from their sharing, but their projects have garnered thousands of hits and many comments on the movie sharing site—gaining them the outside audience I always hoped to get them through past technology projects.

Playing with the films in this way, through the use of technology, allowed the students not only to "game" the assignment but to access rhetorical invention in ways that meme creators often do but students often don't. It sets up their presence as part of a group of students (the *E.T.* group, for example), and changes their fate from one of passive compliance to active resistance to the way that classrooms ordinarily operate. I have also begun to assign this project at Frostburg State University in the Applied Digital Writing course (ENGL438). In that class, students do this project first, but still, however, they then study Gee and gaming rhetorics. They are given an introduction, then, to being immersed as a way of learning and then learn *why* that was done. Since many of the students in our program plan to go on and become teachers this seems to be an effective strategy.

Sweded Movie Project Assignment Sheet

In the movie *Be Kind Rewind,* Jack Black and Mos Def recreate movies using cruddy camera equipment and poorly constructed special effects after an entire video store worth of movies is erased in a freak "magnetic man" accident. They refer to this process as "sweding," and sweding has become a bit of an Internet phenomenon.

For this project, you will be working with a group to create a script for a sweded film. Although in the movie no script was required, this is—unfortunately—a class and so you will be expected to put some degree of thought into your project.

Here is your grading criteria:

1. Length—movie should be between 3–5 minutes. Any longer and you're working too hard (although it may be acceptable). 25 points

2. Theme/Argument—the movie should convey the same basic points as the original. 50 points

3. Script—you need to write a script. 25 points

4. Group paper—You should write a paper (detailed below) describing the rhetorical decisions you've made, changes you had to make to the script, etc. 100 points

5. Extra Credit—Post to YouTube

So, here's what you need to do:

1. Pick a movie with your group that you believe you can recreate using existing camera equipment (cell phones, cameras you own, or mine in class).

2. Make a list of the scenes you believe are necessary to convey the basic mood, theme, and argument of the movie. Be prepared to defend your choices.

3. Write a script and think of common everyday items that you could use to convey the scene, characters, and props necessary to the movie. Collect them.

4. Practice, if necessary.

5. Film.

6. Edit—though not too much. It's fun to look professional, but remember that you can look *unprofessional* and leave in mistakes, that's part of the fun of sweding. Editing can be done on Windows Movie Maker, iMovie, Adobe Premiere, Adobe After Effects, Final Cut Pro, or other free software.

7. Write about it. I recommend taking notes throughout to make this part easier. Your group only needs to turn in one essay.

Your essay should contain:

1. What you believe the central theme and argument of your chosen movie is.

2. The scenes, costumes, filming locations, and other things that convey the theme or argument of the movie

3. You probably should write at *least* seven to eight pages in order to do this well.

In some classrooms, it may be necessary to review safety rules with students when refilming big-budget movies. Some students (especially nontraditional ones, in my experience) want to make things as "realistic" as possible, which has ended in me having classroom rules like "no real fire" and "no locking anyone, ever, for any reason, in the trunk of your car." I require a script to be turned in before students can use class time for filming, and I must know where they are and what they are doing at all times. They must not disturb other classes, and they must seek permission from campus police if anything they are doing might alert them. If they do want to do something dangerous, we talk about ways to use things like forced perspective, models, and even editing software like Adobe AfterEffects to make the project instead of turning their classmates into stunt people.

Despite those somewhat scary sounding rules, this is my favorite project. Student engagement is always high. After introducing the assignment, I show them videos from past classes, and they are usually determined to become a good example for the next term. At least one group (when taught at a diverse school) will usually find that they cannot cast their movie without bending genders and races, which results in papers that are critical of Hollywood's representation of characters in terms of gender and race. That sets up wonderful conversations later in the class about culture and media.

The Community Project (ENGL438, Frostburg State University)

In my senior-level digital writing course (ENGL438), students are asked to study an online community. They are asked to look into how it operates, what the rules are, how people treat one another, and how they deal with conflict. They have to identify sites of conflict in the past, read through them, and rhetorically analyze them. What forms of rhetoric are present? Not present? Does the site have its own slang? Acronyms? Memes?

To do this, students are taught how to do coding for ethnographic field notes (in general, this is not necessary for the game project if taught at a lower level, but becomes necessary here as a student might be going through hundreds of pages of posts). I show them how to save those posts as PDF files and use the Kindle App or a different PDF annotation app to code them. I also show them what that would look like on paper. We look at how to make spreadsheets to make sense out of data, select quotes for inclusion into their papers, and how to properly anonymize names.

Students are then also asked, briefly, to post to the community and see what happens. We talk—a lot—about how this is not part of normal ethnographic research. However, if they have done a good job of learning about the community they should be able to post without immediately being labeled as a "newb." In one case, a student was upset about the way that gay people were being talked about on one forum and was able to make a positive change in the way the conversation was going by posting a lot of Madonna pictures—she included that conversation in an Appendix because she was quite proud.

From the project students learn that every community is different. What "works" rhetorically in one space online might not work in another. Since some of our students go on to work in PR, I believe this is an important lesson to learn even if it is completely divorced from my own research.

Throughout the process I also monitor students to ensure that their "intrusions" are ethical. Thus far, however, there have been no problems. Most post a picture or introduction or comment on a few threads and are welcomed warmly.

Final Term Project Assignment Sheet
(ENGL438, Applied Digital Writing)

For your final term paper, you will be exploring an Internet community in order to discuss a wide variety of readings and topics covered in the class. By the end of the term we will have discussed many different theories of digital games, systems, databases, graphics, and new media. Your job will be to summarize and analyze those theories in relation to one online community of your choosing. How do the works we've read relate to the community? Does the community disprove any of the readings? Support them? Complicate them? How do the community members deal with identity, conflict, and argument?

First step: Find an online community to study. Any community will do, but it will be helpful if you can identify a past or current conflict. It will also be helpful if you are interested in the issues of the community yourself. Communities that have a complete searchable history are best so that you can study how the community has developed, how rules have changed, etc. over time. Examples: Reddit (specifically certain subreddits), Feministe, Livejournal, 4Chan (they have an archive), I can haz cheeseburger, Equestria Daily, Ponychan, Metafilter, Schnoogle, etc.

Second step: Start reading and saving text. In order to properly code your research, you will need copies if not print outs of all the text you read. Yes, this sort of sucks but it is how it is done. We will talk about doing this sort of research and coding in class.

Third Step: Consider all the readings from this term (and any I recommend to you based upon your topic as well as any you find on your own), what connections, analyses, and even disconnects can you find between the theory and what you experienced in the community. Also consider rhetorical theory, critical theory, and anything else you have read or discovered through other courses.

Fourth Step: Post to the community. Attempt to post a controversial opinion. Please do so under a pseudonym registered under an email address that does not use your name (not your university e-mail). Try to change someone's opinion, based upon what you know about the site and how people treat one another. Were you successful? Why or why not?

Fifth: Write! Paper should be between 15–20 pages long. If you need to include excessively long quotes they should be included in an appendix or not count towards page count. The paper should be in MLA or APA format. In-text citation is required for reading sources as well as research sites. Additionally, you should introduce ALL sources as if classmates and other readers do not already know them.

This project is most interesting to students who plan to attend graduate school or those who are going into public relations, in terms of future work, but can be useful outside of class as well. Unlike the other projects listed here, this is one that can help students navigate online communities in thoughtful ways rather than just diving in and beginning to post. It encourages the online behavior of "lurking" before posting, which is generally considered to be an internet best practice anyway. However, in a world where accounts can be created and created again, I have noticed a downturn in students reading a lot before beginning to communicate on a site, Facebook Group, or even class community. Thoughtful reflection on how ad-hocs work online can benefit students who grew up with these as part of their natural environment.

Augmented Reality Project (ENGL438, Frostburg State University)

In the Augmented Reality project, my students in my senior digital writing course are asked to create displays for an Augmented Reality app named Aurasma. This app allows you to connect virtual material (pictures and video) to real-world objects in real space. For example, if you point the app, which runs on your phone, at a sign in my classroom, it plays a video that looks like a monster is crawling out of it (we downloaded the monster). There is also a sign by my door that will play an animation about one of the episodes of the podcast *Welcome to Nightvale*, and there are signs in the Lane Center (like a Union building) on campus that will tell you more about the gym and the bookstore.

Students have two options for this project—one is to add value to things on campus to make them more fun or to make an argument. The other is to add value to things on or off campus to inform. In the first year that I taught this project nearly all of my students wanted to partner with the local museum to create interactive museum displays. In the second year, nearly all of them wanted to put up hidden information all around campus (and much of that hidden information was vaguely trollish).

Aurasma is wonderfully easy to use and could be taught at any level. I teach it, for my seniors, alongside object-orientated ontology, and the write up they are required to do reflects that. However, it could be taught in any number of other ways, including as part of a visual rhetoric or design unit.

Augmented Reality Project Assignment Sheet

For this project, you will be using ready-made software to tie pictures, text, and websites to sites in the real world via Augmented Reality (AR).

AR is used to play games and post information in real space that can be viewed via a mobile device or heads-up display.

In this project you will be working with one of the following spaces:

1. Frostburg State Campus

2. City of Frostburg.

3. Frostburg Museum

4. Museum in the Gunther Museum

5. Rocky Gap State Park

6. Or Other Approved Site

In this space you will be linking text, pictures, etc. to real spaces to tell stories. If you are working in a museum those stories, audio messages, text, etc. should be ones that are related to the artifacts and real. On campus you can choose to build a game or tell a real story.

You may choose to work with either a departmental iPad or your own mobile device, but your device must have a camera and be able to recognize parts of your environment. Some devices require that you post a small shape, QR code, or picture for AR to work, so be sure to match a good device with a space it will work in.

Grading:	
Spelling/Grammar/etc.	25 points
Appropriateness	25 points
Development	25 points
Creativity	25 points

The project's goal is to get you thinking in a way that uses space rhetorically. These sorts of displays are getting more popular for museums (cheaper and more interactive than guides) and so are another potential source of post-school employment as well! AR is also used in building alternate reality games, making apps for exercise, and zombie simulations.

Students nearly always report that augmented reality is "cool." Students who worked for the newspaper, particularly, enjoyed getting to make part of it look like a newspaper from *Harry Potter*. Prior to 2016–2017, buy-in, however, was difficult beyond those students. I had argued for several years that augmented reality would be the "next thing" and would be a valuable tool to have when searching for work, but students were not so sure. Fortunately, with the development of *Pokémon Go*, my students at last recognize the value and fun intrinsic to this system.

In previous years, I had attempted to get students to play *Ingress* (2013), which is an augmented reality game that pre-dates *Pokémon Go*, was made by the same company, and even features the same locations. Students were not as excited by *Ingress* (2013), however, because it did not feature a narrative they were already familiar with. Most of the fun of *Pokémon Go* (2016) is not traveling from place to place, it is in collecting Pokémon that students already know about from watching the television show or playing other Pokémon games. As a result, starting in Spring 2017 students will be required to play *Pokémon Go* (2016) and write about the experience as an introduction to this project and will have to think of ways to incorporate more known narratives into their work.

Group blogs (OAD121, ENG3010, Baker College, Wayne State University)

I have also begun to examine the ways that our classroom technology usage fails to fit in with the way the larger Internet is used as a whole. A change that I've made has been to class blogs. Blogs seem like a wonderful idea, but engender much student resistance. In short—they just don't write them, or if they do, they are very short. They hate having to go read each other's and leave comments, and even if I force them to, it's pretty obvious that the writing is forced.

The most popular blogs online often have more than one author and have been slowly transforming themselves into media networks over the past decade. They put all these varying peoples' opinions in one place, which means that discussion is often furious and long. Furthermore, they don't shut down every couple months and start over like many personal blogs do—they have a long history and an archive available for people to pick up and read if they want to catch up or understand the viewpoints of some posters better. The blog doesn't disappear even when the entire cast of writers changes over—it is still there, still being published, and still has an audience.

When I was teaching OAD121 (Office Procedures and Technologies 1 for Administrative Assistants at Baker College of Allen Park), I created a group blog and had each student create a username on it. They could post and read on the same site, and were allowed to cite one another in their final papers. This worked relatively well. The next term, I then added the new students, and so on. They were allowed to go back and read what other people had said about past prompts. Old students often commented on new students' posts. They were in conversation with people who had finished the program and were working in the real world about what things were really like versus what their book had to say about them. Then, because the blog had a lot of activity, people from the outside started looking in as well.

While that first group of students did not see the immediate effects of the new blog style, they did eventually communicate with future students in the course and were able to share their experiences as experts. Some of them chose to gently tease the new students about how wonderful life was after college. I no longer teach the class, but see that comments are still being posted from time to time, although many of the students have moved their posting over to Facebook and have added people that they met through the blog (and, from what I understand, this lead to at least one person getting a job where an older student already worked).

What this type of blog does (that others do not) is that it places students into a larger, anonymous community that is much like an ad-hoc. They are working together to create knowledge, and while I still worked at those schools it was not unusual for old students to come back and comment on new students' work or respond to their comments. That never happened in small class blogs, so this larger one seems to be an answer to some of the problems I had with blogs previously as a student and teacher (and the anonymity helps).

Five Second Films (ENGL438, Frostburg State University)

One alternative that I have developed to the sweding project is to have students create "5 Second Films." This is a genre of movie that has developed on YouTube, with one group of actors and artists (posting at http://5secondfilms.com/) developing a new one each day. In this type of video, an entire story is told in just five seconds of video. In many ways, these are the multimedia variant of the famous challenge to write the shortest story possible, to which Hemingway (supposedly, though the story is also credited to other writers in some versions of the tale) wrote: "Baby shoes for sale. Never worn."

The challenge for students is to communicate as much as possible in as little time as possible. These videos are intensely intertextual, calling upon people's knowledge of other stories, tv shows, movies, and books in order to make sense. Without cultural knowledge, people can neither understand nor make such a video.

Filming and editing for these projects is very quick, so most of the time is spent coming up with a concept and then figuring out how to tell it quickly.

Five Second Movies Assignment Sheet

Your first assignment is to script, film, and edit a very short movie. 5 Second Films have become popular on YouTube, and will be the first form of new media/multimedia that we examine this term.

A five second film, as a genre, tells an entire story in a very short period of time. This idea is not new; in fact, there is a famous anecdote that Hemmingway created the first six-word story: Baby shoes for sale. Never worn.

Your movie is going to function very similarly. You must use cultural tropes, allusions to other media and movies, and your audience's general knowledge of a topic in order to tell a story in five seconds. Your audience fills in the rest. No, not everyone will get the exact same story out of your film—this is one of the reasons that some people regard new media and multimedia as an art form rather than a standard form of human communication.

The "five seconds" refers to five seconds of action, not including titles, ads and credits. Swearing is allowed, nudity and porn are not. Please do not endanger others through acts such as riding kayaks down stairs, lighting things/people on fire, knives, guns, etc. When filming on campus you must follow all campus/University rules and guidelines.

Grading	
Story	25 points
Script	5 points
Explanation/Cultural Significance	50 points
Editing	20 points

My favorite project from this assignment was a fake commercial for Barbie wherein two girls hold up their new Barbies and say, "I have Cthulhu Barbie!" and another says "I have Zombie Barbie!" and then the first girl says, "Let's make them. . . ." and it cuts to the Barbie logo with a bleep. In addition to being very happy to have had a Cthulhu Barbie made in my class, this and other projects showed that students understood how to take people's experiences and use them to fill in gaps.

Schopenhauer Alternative Rhetorical Analysis (ENGL438, Frostburg State University)

For this project, students study *The Art of Controversy* as part of the advanced digital writing course. Earlier in the course they will have already completed a traditional rhetorical analysis. For this project, they choose a new piece of media (it does not have to be a movie—it can be writing, a video, or anything else, though I encourage them to pick an argument) to analyze using Schopenhauer's work instead of traditional rhetoric.

Though not explicitly a political assignment, students who are already political will usually choose a debate or politician's writing for the project. Others enjoy tearing apart arguments online (especially if we are not doing the project about online communities that term) or arguments between characters in books, television, or movies. The only issue with choosing some media is that the argument must be long with several different "rhetorical" moves to generate enough information for the paper, so I ask for topics early in the process to make sure they will work.

Alternative Rhetorical Analysis Assignment Sheet

For this assignment, you will be using the reading we have recently completed, Schopenhauer's *The Art of Controversy*, to analyze an argument of your choosing. The first part of this project is going to be to identify an argument where you recognize the types of rhetorical moves that Schopenhauer uses—I recommend that you look online, on television, and in writing if you cannot immediately think of something. I will ask you to share your chosen argument during an upcoming class session.

Second, you must prepare a paper (6–8 pages) that describes how some of the rhetorical moves that Schopenhauer proposes are present in the argument that you have chosen. Analyze much as you would in the earlier rhetorical analysis. Ultimately, who wins the argument? Why? What can we learn from this process?

The concluding section of your paper needs to compare this analysis to how a traditional rhetorical analysis of this argument would work. What do you learn about rhetoric through this process?

Grading	
Use of Schopenhauer	15
Organization	10
Development	25
Spelling/Grammar	25
Comparison to Tradition- al Rhetoric	25

The best of these assignments are either very serious, or not serious at all. Students who are already very politically active can write wonderful reviews of the ways politicians use fallacies and elements of Schopenhauer's rhetorical devices in their debates and public writing. Conversely, a student who plans to work with young children did this assignment and used it to analyze preschool children's arguments. The paper was adorable, but also intriguing.

The Alternate Reality Class (ENGL330, Frostburg State University)

During my first year at Frostburg State University, I worked with a team of professors and graduate students at other schools (Doug Eyman, Wendi Sierra, Mary Karcher, Emi Bunner, Sheryl Ruskiewicz, Anthony Harrison, and Scott Reed) to create an Alternate Reality Game for students. In this game, my students (enrolled in ENGL330, Business Writing) would be helping to create game materials that would be played by students at the other schools. Alternate reality games (ARGs) blend real-life items, places, people, and media with video game elements to tell an immersing story (Szulborski, 2005). ARGs do their best to try to convince players that they are not games. They use real-world technology instead of just "screens" as much as possible in order to convince players of such. In past ARGs, players would solve puzzles that lead them to go to a specific pay phone at a specific time on a specific day to be there when the phone rang and so that they could hear a message. That would then be shared with other players via message boards set up by players for themselves. ARGs have been used primarily as tools for advertising, but sometimes are now used in education and just for fun. The most famous ones have tended to be used for advertising other games, and have the power, creativity, and financial backing of large corporations. Deciding to replace this with a team of students was only a little crazy, it turned out.

For our ARG that we titled "Glen is Dead," students enrolled in freshman composition classes at Baker College (where I used to work) would be invited to participate in an online internship program with Rove, Lacier, and Piton, a small think-tank whose name happened to be an anagram of Evil Incorporated. When the term started, we had plotted out a decent chunk of the story, and my students would be the ones writing letters to the students at other schools inviting them to join. If they chose to participate in the internship program, they would gain access not only to research materials from the company but also be able to participate in studies, use databases, and have people from the company (my students) help them with their writing. It was a humanitarian project, after all. My students would get practice writing real business documents for a real audience, and many of their documents would also be posted to the Web. They also scripted videos, some of which were filmed by classmates and some by professors at other schools. In turn, the freshmen would get their writing read and developed by advanced students in other states, gaining a wider audience online but still a safe one.

To get started, in the story, Doug Eyman's character Glen was bit by a rabid Pomeranian infected with the zombie virus (played by my dog, Riddle) and the rest was history—we started the Zombie apocalypse.

Of course, students caught on that this was no normal "internship" right away. Why would a company be interested in their research? We had to let them in on the "story" fairly early in the term, which was not part of our original plan. However, that did not keep my students from writing to them and even wanting to change the end of the story that we had pre-written. They also worked on giving feedback to the freshmen at the other school, and the freshmen gave them feedback on their business writing as well. Students also produced videos and web materials that made the company more "real."

A fuller description of this project was published in *Play/Write*, published by Parlor Press in 2016.

THE MOOC IDEA (NOWHERE, YET)

MOOCS (Massively Open Online Courses) have largely not made good on their promise to democratize education by allowing everyone to learn. Part of the problem is that not everyone who enrolls in a MOOC can earn credit, and that companies (and schools) do not always recognize MOOC credit as valid.

Taking what I have learned from the Alternate Reality Game in Business Writing, I would like to create a MOOC that uses Alternate Reality (and Augmented Reality) to immerse students in a story, and also set up a winning condition under which some students can receive credit.

The idea is this: Alternate Reality Games ask people to travel to locations, work together, answer phones, solve puzzles, do research, and generally do a lot of real world work all for a small prize (getting to play a game early, for example). They put a story on top of what would largely be a bunch of busy work if people did not want to solve the puzzle. Augmented reality could be used to hide things in plain sight around the school the game is hosted at (to get students to visit campus and consider enrolling) as well as in other parts of the country and digitally to make sure that students who are enrolled everywhere get a chance to be important and help out their team.

MOOCs face a problem wherein a lot of students drop out and only a few finish. Why is this? I believe one reason is that without a physical classroom or *some other reason to continue to participate* many people simply cannot commit class time. An engaging storyline and group that is depending on you, on the other hand, might create exactly the sort of engagement that people need to be successful in a MOOC.

Second, using Alternate Reality to immerse people sets up the class as a game. Since games have winning conditions, a certain number of people enrolled (players) could win each and every term—and that "win" could be real college credit. While some would no doubt transfer that credit elsewhere, some would probably be people who are interested in going to the school where the game is hosted, so the game could also be a recruiting tool for the university. I also imagine that the "winners" would have their work reviewed by professors (instead of classmates and computers). This would reduce the workload on the professors who develop the course but guarantee that the winners have actually done college quality work before they receive credit.

While this has not yet been developed, if I am encouraged to develop a MOOC for my institution, this is the one that I wish to build. I believe that competition in such courses is necessary and healthy. Some paid MOOCs already use this principle: for example, MOOCs on *Master-Class* offer students the opportunity to have their work read or seen by a famous artist, writer, or movie producer if it is good enough.

Going Beyond the Classroom

In most of these assignments, I attempt to make a connection to materials that exist outside of class. Especially in senior-level courses, I want students thinking about how they can use technology skills after class, but also want to ensure that they develop critical thinking that helps them analyze digital media that does not use traditional rhetorical means after graduation.

Ideally, I would like to see students use these tools that they are given to go out and make positive changes that they want to see in the world (digital and otherwise). There are many theories about how they can do that, from using games to encourage participation in communities to learning how to use play to become more creative. For now, I hope to give students new skills in understanding and creating digital media as part of my classes, but others have created games that they hope to use to engage communities in improvement.

Reality Is Broken

In Jane McGonigal's 2011 publication *Reality is Broken: Why Games Make Us Better and How They Can Change the World*, McGonigal (a game designer and theorist) writes about why games are so engaging for people but also postulates why and how we should change the world to be more like them since they are fulfilling to almost everyone who tries them (unlike our real-world jobs and lives). Gamers, she notes, want to find a section of reality that is just as engaging, that makes them feel alive, that gives them heroic power, community, success, and failure, as games do. After all, their favorite games give them all these things all the time, and that is why they choose to spend as much time in them as they do.

McGonigal writes that games are filling some of our very real human needs that our real lives simply do not. Whether playing *World of Warcraft* or *Candy Crush* or even *Bejeweled Blitz* or *Farmville*, gamers get something out of the game that their real life simply cannot give them. In games we earn rewards, we are inspired, and we are engaged. They also manage to bring us together in ways that reality does not (2011).

I feel that it is necessary to point out here, as McGonigal (2011) does, that many people think that games are escapist and therefore bad for us. However, games can and should be seen as a sort of purposeful escape—if we are spending so many hours playing games there is a good chance that our own lives have become broken in some way (and our own schools have become so as well) and that *not* playing games will not fix that.

She believes that rather than throwing ourselves into virtual worlds that we can and should be creating game-like elements that play out in the real world—we can use games to fix reality, and a lot of game designers agree with her (McGonigal, 2011). Rather than escaping or giving up our games entirely, there is a middle road that is neither lazy nor escapist nor depressing—we can game the world. She would like to see those who know how to make games or recognize where they happen to begin to focus on the task of making our real lives the best that they can be and for as many people as possible. Rather than turning us off from reality, tomorrow's games could increase our engagement with it and enable us to make ever greater connections with others and the world as well.

Some people continue to write off games as not being worth our time and study. Our media actually helps this (not least of all because they have something to lose when people stop watching the news and television shows and start playing *WoW* instead) by continuously reporting that the reason that children are obese is not because of sociological problems like poverty and changing the BMI scale, but is instead because they are playing too many games. Unfortunately, according to McGonigal, the folks who continue to believe that games are useless and evil will miss out on learning how to leverage the power that games give us in their own communities. Of course, writing teachers are always the ones that want to keep something like that from occurring. Thus, it is not surprising that games and their connection to writing and learning are increasingly discussed at conferences like the College Conference on Composition and Communication (CCCC's), which makes it much easier to understand why I overheard someone asking at *Computers and Writing* 2010 "Wait, isn't this Computers and Writing? Because it seems like we should start calling it Games and Writing." There were several panels that were about gaming, there was a game room, and publishers were sponsoring prizes for being good at those games.

In trying to solve the problems that newcomers of the College Conference of Composition and Communication might have, I worked on a conference game with several other graduate students and faculty members across the country. This game gives rewards to newcomers for doing things they should be doing anyway (meeting publishers, attending parties, networking with other players, talking about programs, talking about teaching, attending a variety of panels, and even finding out where all the free food and alcohol is). By attaching a reward to doing these things, we can assure that players who might be too shy to talk with some people or attend some panels will do so—and that is the goal of the game.

Most people would not assume that *this* game is a waste of your time (of course, you could do all these things without playing, but who really does?), but we do dismiss many games as a waste of time. However, McGonigal argues that games can help teach us about our true selves (2011). In its first version, that conference game that I helped build several years ago now asks players to determine whether they are most interested in becoming professors, administrators, or publishers and then has them follow a path to find out more about those things at the conference. Later versions allowed all players to complete all quests. Games help us think about ourselves and our strengths and develop our weaknesses. They ask us to think, to organize, and to act.

In designing such a game, we had to consider how to be a leader in this community of scholars for anybody who was playing. We had to think of ways to force players to work together to win prizes. We had to build in ways for them to achieve agency in what might very well be a very strange and overwhelming space.

Our reality may be broken, as McGonigal notes, but games provide us a way to fix it. She wants us to begin to create ways to connect with reality better, rather than dissociate from it (2011). Games can be used to tackle real dilemmas (like racism) and improve real people's lives. Games do not have to ask us to abandon our own ethics and morals and substitute someone else's rules if they are open ended enough to allow multiple outcomes. Furthermore, we should be able to volunteer to play games or not, and that in and of itself means that we should not have to give up our morals to play by someone else's rules.

Games ask us to fix unnecessary obstacles, according to McGonigal (2011). They ask us to solve problems we do not have to solve, and always give us more problems to choose to solve than we really can. They give us interesting problems with arbitrary limitations to make the play more interesting (chess would be too easy if any piece could go anywhere, and it would be impossible to win). Games give us interesting and entertaining feedback whether we are doing well or poorly.

If anything, anyone that has become a graduate student or professor should understand why unnecessary obstacles that we choose to take on make us happy, or, at the very least, understand that they do. No one really needs a PhD. No one really needs to write a three-hundred-page paper. Yet, we take these challenges on for ourselves and are happy when our best students make this choice as well. Did anyone ever really say, "You know, I have to understand Heidegger to make my life complete"? No, they probably didn't. We are the perfect community to understand the idea that unnecessary obstacles keep our brains happy and engaged in ways that necessary ones often do not.

According to McGonigal (2011), the reason these things make us happy is because they are hard work that we have chosen for ourselves. People truly are happy when they have good, hard work to do. She notes that the opposite of playing is not working—it is depression, and we are a far more depressed society than at nearly any other historical time period. According to the DSM IV definition of depression, we have a sense of inadequacy and are despondent and lack activity (as cited in McGonigal, 2011). When we play a game we experience the opposite state. Games allow us to think positively, build personal strengths, and we even condition our minds and bodies to be happier—something that our jobs really do not often do.

McGonigal argues that our jobs should be giving us this kind of input and challenge. People are increasingly unhappy with their work, and that should not be the case. People turn to games, to online communities, and to places like 4Chan and Anonymous to give them the input and voluntary obstacles that peoples' jobs fail to give them. Jobs can and should give people customizable "missions" and real-time interesting feedback (McGonigal, 2011). Humans enjoy "hard fun," and if our jobs and our schools gave us that we would be less likely to seek out video games. Game designers believe that people must have *fiero* (pride) in what they do, and often times we fail to reach that state in our normal day-to-day lives (McGonigal, 2011). Games are already being used to make chores more fun and rewarding (via an ARG called *ChoreMaster*) and air travel less stressful via games like Ian Bogost's *JetSet* and inflight trivia games.

If this, and even what Gee describes in schools and in life, seems utterly impossible, don't be so sure. McGonigal describes a school that opened in 2009 called Quest that does not use games to teach; instead, the entire school is a game built on the logic of MMORPGs (2011). Students at Quest, in New York, might find hidden puzzles in library books that will earn them extra points for completing them, have "boss battles" where they have to work in teams and make use of the special skills they've developed, and are asked not only to work on subjects that they aren't very good in, but to develop further the skills that they are good at. They are not graded so much as they "level up," which is a more egalitarian system than traditional grading because if you are not good at something you can continue working on it until you become good at it. This makes failure less disappointing and more challenging and means that succeeding leads you to take on bigger and harder tasks rather than accepting your A and going home (McGonigal, 2011).

When reading about such a system I cannot help but be reminded of two things in college writing instruction: (1) Our present traditional trend in grading—reintroducing bell curves, a focus on correctness, and standardized syllabi and (2) our complaints against entitled students who just do not seem to care about our classes and assignments. Students do not seem to work very hard, are worried about getting it "right" (when in writing there rarely is one right way to complete an assignment) and just want to get assignments and classes done and over with. We know that this is not the proper way to get a degree or learn, but what can we do when our best efforts at making people care doesn't really seem to work?

Traditional education can adapt to better engage students who are more used to playing games and being engaged with on a very high level when not at school or work. Assignments like the sweded video project that ask students to play with ideas are one decent step at doing this. We also need to create classes where assignments are more open-ended—not less. The current back to basics, standardization push is unlikely to permanently help many of our students except those that find education to be a voluntary challenge to begin with (and we, as professors and graduate students, probably already fall into that group). We have to give them other voluntary challenges. One of the reasons the video project works is that they can work with any movie that they want to—they choose how hard or how easy the movie they want to remake will be. They decide whether to have to dress up, whether to be in front of the camera, whether to use toys to do stop motion animation—in short, they get to decide what sort of challenge they want. Since the work can be done in a group or alone, they also get to make that choice for themselves. This sort of voluntary challenge means that whatever work they do decide to take on is the one that they want.

One of my deepest concerns about our current movement in Composition and Rhetoric is that we will fail to take advantage of the real ways we can engage with and teach our students and instead continue to try to force them into an outdated standard of "the way things are done" because that is, on the surface, easier to assess. As a program director, I can attest to the fact that a standardized curriculum is easier to assess, but at the same time, the best work that I see out of every class I have collected data on rarely comes from the standard assignments. Instead, when teachers develop innovative assignments that allow students to play with concepts and leave them many potential paths to completion, the work is outstanding, the students are happy, and the teachers cannot wait to show it off. What more could an instructor want?

Play as Rhetorical Invention

I believe that play is one way to introduce rhetorical invention to the classroom. When I first stumbled upon 4Chan and Anonymous, realizing that the lack of censorship in these communities led to widespread invention, remixing, and play with ideas identified for me one of many things that was wrong with my own use of technology in my classroom. One way that humans create is through play. We play make believe as children and come up with stories. We develop moves and strategies by playing sports. We eventually learn that there is a perfect technique for playing *Ms. PacMan* through playing—not watching, not reading. We can understand, in theory, exactly how to do something on a computer, but until we "play with it" we will likely still not be able to understand the actions we have to take as well as we would like to.

Play and games, as well as admitting that the Internet as a whole is a kind of game, is an intervention that our classrooms need. Clay Shirky (2010) writes that we are lousy at predicting what new technologies actually can do for us. We cannot determine, until we are using them and *playing* with them, what a new communication tool is actually good for. If that's true, now that the Internet is in common use we need to seriously take another look at this technology and think seriously about what is working on it and what is not.

What *works* is procedural rhetorics and play, what 4Chan and Anonymous and fandoms have created for us. We have a choice—we can recreate small bits of this game in our classrooms, or we can put our students into the Game of the Internet by having them create memes, introduce them to the Internet community, and play with things that are already made. While I'm perfectly happy having my students make Lolcats as an assignment, that feels less authentic than getting them to come up with their own image macros. If something like Privilege Denying Dude can catch on enough to shut down a Tumblr account (and indeed, if they had not shut it down, it would have likely dropped their entire service), then a meme that my students come up with that makes fun of a common occurrence in their own lives is just as likely to gain momentum. If it did that would be a rhetorical triumph.

Because new media has become part of our common lives now does not mean that we can stop relooking at it and re-determining how to best teach argumentation via it. "Creating the most value from a tool involves not master plans or great leaps forward but constant trial and error" (Shirky, 2010, p. 191). We need to learn to get more out of the process of these shifts, because there are groups of *players* out there who are already doing so. If the Internet can be treated as a game and doing so makes you a better rhetorician then that is the process that we should be undergoing in our classes.

Of course, such gaming systems in classrooms will have problems; however, "as a general rule, it is more important to try something new, and work on the problems as they arise, than to figure out a way to do something new without having any problems" (Shirky, 2010, p. 205). Rather than being afraid of attempting new pedagogies and assignments, I have begun to introduce the new at every turn that I can. What has been the result? A happier instructor and happier students who write better assignments. The Game of the Internet has taught me that something rarely becomes viral years after it was created. Likewise, is it with technology assignments. Waiting until something is no longer fresh to bring it to my classroom will not make my students as happy as showing them the new now.

A CONCLUSION TO THE CONCLUSION

Of course, I cannot end this discussion without reminding the reader that the Game of the Internet is not always a positive or inclusive space. 4Chan and Anonymous, the creators of the Game, primarily use it for annoyance, harassment, and now hacktivism (although they are getting "better" at using their game for what we generally consider to be good ends). We have a great deal of what Shirky refers to as "cognitive surplus," and we have to decide how to use it. Giving students complete freedom in the creation of online communities for themselves might well lead to the creation of something like 4Chan itself. To make these classroom-appropriate we must carefully monitor and moderate the unmoderatable to create something that looks more like a *My Little Pony* fan community or Privilege Denying Dude—not an easy task.

But the Game of the Internet *does not have to be a negative, racist, or sexist space.* It is not, by definition, any of these. It is a *fun* space, and one with rules that lend themselves to viral messages and play, but it is not a hate-filled space by definition.

We have a cognitive surplus, and we must decide whether we will use some of it to either educate our students or allow them to educate themselves as they continue using their free time to play the Game of the Internet or fan games, joining what Shirky calls the Invisible University (2010). We can let the Game stay as it is today, or we can begin to play as well. Our input will matter, if we choose to play, and we can inject the public and civic value that we wish was there (as long as we don't try too hard and create a forced meme—but no matter). This will not be an easy task, but it is one that I think is worth undertaking.

Can we afford to continue to let the people who are at the bleeding edge of using the Internet be the people who make sexist and racist jokes just because they are offensive? Or can we use the systems that they have designed and the Game that they have set up to get the most of out of our technology? Shirky (2010) notes that we can get what we want out of the Internet, but we have to make it. We cannot simply sit back and be passive observers. Likewise, we cannot use the Internet as we have in the past in our classrooms and continue to have assignments fail or fail to engage students—doing so will mean that our students not only will fail to learn but also that we too will submit to ennui and boredom and begin to spend more of our time away from the jobs we love.

Swarms and ad-hocs are tremendously powerful tools. They are currently being used both to fight fascism and authoritarianism but also to help build it. There are ad-hocs that are extremely liberal, but also many that are extremely conservative. No matter which side you are on, ignoring the power of these systems would be dangerous.

We cannot afford to continue to ignore that "those kids online" are doing things that might well affect world politics. Nicola Griffith (2016) writes that swarms can help defeat autocrats and take back control. Anonymity can be a great tool. We are in a historical moment not just in the

United States but in many countries where digital rhetoric when used procedurally by large crowds can make a real difference in the world. That difference deserves the voices of students and teachers to be added to it.

We have to take advantage of the crowd. We have to recognize that more is different, and that we need to get our students out onto the *real* Internet and away from our safe Blackboard classes if we want to experience that within our students' rhetorical education.

In games, we often want to create or defend utopia. But in the Game of the Internet, there is no utopia, there is no safe space. We have to come out of our safe spaces and begin to live the game instead. As Wark writes:

> In gamespace, the very possibility of utopia is foreclosed. It is no longer possible to describe a shining city upon the hill, as if it were a special topic untouched by the everyday, workaday world. No space is sacred: no space is separate. Not even the space of the page. The gamelike extends its line everywhere and nowhere. (Wark, 2007, p. 102)

Games are curious and critical, but they are not perfect. They are not non-violent. The Game of the Internet is no different. Rather than escaping into gamespace from the everyday, we should recognize and augment the gamespace *in* the everyday. The Game of the Internet does this, and its success is partially based upon making a game out of what we already do. We must, then, collaborate, recognize procedurality where we find it, and mutate amenable spaces into games if we are to remain rhetorically sufficient into the future.

References

4Chan. (2007–2015). *4Chan*. Retrieved from http://www.4chan.org

4Chan. (2011). /b/ Random. *4Chan*. Retrieved from http://www.4chan.org/b/

5 Second Films. (2008). 5 Second Films. *5 Second Films*. Retrieved from http://5secondfilms.com/

Alexander, L. (2014, August 28). "Gamers" don't have to be your audience. "Gamers" are over. *Gamasutra*. Retrieved from http://archive.is/l1kTW

Alexander, S. (1923, Octoboer-November). Dr. Johnson as a Philosopher. *Cornhill magazine*. LV, 385-92, 513-22.

Andersen, D. (2013, March 13). Anonymous participate in silent protest as Steubenville rape trial starts. *Cleveland.com*. Retrieved from http://www.cleveland.com/metro/index.ssf/2013/03/anonymous_participate_in_silen.html

Argumentum ad tldr. (2015). In *RationalWiki*. Retrieved from http://rationalwiki.org/wiki/Gish_Gallop#Argumentum_ad_tl.3Bdr

Astley, R. (1987). Never gonna give you up. [Song]. *Whenever you need somebody*. California: RCA Records.

Atari, Inc. (1981). *Video pinball*. [Video game]. Atari.

Atari, Inc. (1982). *Centipede*. [Video game]. Atari.

Atari, Inc. (1982). *Pacman*. [Video game]. Atari.

Avedon, E. & Sutton-Smith, B. (1971). *The Study of games*. Mountain View, California: Ishi Press.

Balsamo, A. (1995). *Technologies of the gendered body: Reading cyborg women*. Durham, NC: Duke University Press Books.

Barnes, K, Marateo, R., & Pixy Ferris, S. (2007). Teaching and Learning with the Net Generation. Retrieved from http://www.ajhepworth.yolasite.com/resources/Teaching_and_Learning_with_the_Net_Generation.pdf

Barthes, R. (1987). The death of the author. *UbuWeb*. Retrieved from http://www.tbook.constantvzw.org/wp-content/death_authorbarthes.pdf

Bateson, B. (1972). "A Theory of Play and Fantasy," in *Steps to an Ecology of Mind*. Chicago: University of Chicago Press.

Bateson, G. (1972). *Steps to an Ecology of Mind*. Ballantine, New York.

BB. (2008). Archive of the Biting Beaver. *Wordpress*. Retrieved from https://archiveofthebitingbeaver.wordpress.com/

BBC News. (2007, March 27). Blog death threats spark debate. *BBC News*. Retrieved from http://news.bbc.co.uk/2/hi/technology/6499095.stm

Bell, D., & Hubler, M. T. (2001). The virtual writing center: Developing ethos through mailing list discourse. *Writing Center Journal, 21*(2), 57–78.

Biddle, S. (2012, June 1). This is what happens when Anonymous tries to destroy you. *Gizmodo*. Retrieved from http://gizmodo.com/5914671/this-is-what-happens-when-anonymous-tries-to-destroy-you

Blizzard Entertainment. (2004). *World of Warcraft*. [MMORPG]. Irvine, CA: Blizzard Entertainment.

Bogost, I. (2007). *Persuasive games: The expressive power of video games*. Boston, MA: The MIT Press.

Bogost, I. (2011). Gamification is bullshit. *Ian Bogost*. Retrieved from http://bogost.com/writing/blog/gamification_is_bullshit/

Box Floods. (2013). In *Insurgency Wiki*. Retrieved from http://insurg.in/index.php?title=Ruin_Life_Tactics#Box_Floods

Broderick, R. (2013, October 22). Meet the men's rights activist who left an Ohio University student too scared to leave her house. *Buzzfeed*. Retrieved from http://www.buzzfeed.com/ryanhatesthis/this-is-what-happens-when-anonymous-accuses-you-of-faking-a#.udMN5DBVe

Caldwell, M. (2013). Anonymous takes on the Maryville rape scandal. Is this a good thing? *Mother Jones*. Retrieved from http://www.motherjones.com/mojo/2013/10/maryville-anonymous-football-rape-case

Chen, A. (2010). Puppy throwing girl caught in Bosnia. *Gawker*. Retrieved from http://gawker.com/5629513/puppy-throwing-girl-caught-in-bosnia

Chin, J. & Wong, G. (2016, November 28). China's new tool for social control: A credit rating for everything. *The Wall Street Journal*. Retrieved from http://www.wsj.com/articles/chinas-new-tool-for-social-control-a-credit-rating-for-everything-1480351590

Cowan, D. (2014, January 8). Daisy Coleman rape case: Maryville teenager's case that divided town to be reviewed. *ABC News Australia*. Retrieved from http://www.abc.net.au/news/2014–01–08/daisy-coleman-rape-case-review-special-prosecutor/5191116

Davidson, A. (2013, March 18). Life after Steubenville. *The New Yorker*. Retrieved from http://www.newyorker.com/news/amy-davidson/life-after-steubenville

Dean, Jodi (2010). *Blog Theory: Feedback and Capture in the Circuits of Drive*. Cambridge, UK: Polity Press.

Dery, M. (1994). *Flame Wars: The discourse of cyberculture*. Durham, NC: Duke University Press Books.

Diaz, J. & Effron, L. (2014, April 3). Newly released documents, Tapes from Maryville teen alleged rape case reveals new details. *ABCNews*. Retrieved from http://abcnews.go.com/US/newly-released-documents-tapes-maryville-teen-alleged-rape/story?id=23164717

Dibbell, J. (1998). A rape in cyberspace: Or TINYSOCIETY, and How to Make One. *My Tiny Life*. Retrieved from http://www.juliandibbell.com/articles/a-rape-in-cyberspace/

Doctorow, C. (2003). *Down and out in the Magic Kingdom*. New York: Tor Books.

Dries, K. (2013, October 23). Maybe Maryville will be different from Steubenville. Here's hoping. *Jezebel*. Retrieved from http://jezebel.com/maybe-maryville-will-be-different-from-steubenville-he-1450657909

Dworkin, A. (2007). *Intercourse*. New York: Basic Books.

Dyer-Witheford, N., de Peuter, G. (2009, December 8). *Games of empire: Global Capitalism and video games*. Minnesota: University of Minnesota Press.

Engel, J. (2012, January 26). Was Socrates a troll? *Quora*. Retrieved from https://www.quora.com/Was-Socrates-a-troll

Ensler, E. (2001). *The Vagina Monologues*. New York: Random House LLC.

Faust, L. (2010). *My Little Pony: Friendship is Magic*. [Television Show]. Pawtucket, Rhode Island: Hasbro.

Fielding, N. & Cobain, I. (2011, March 17). Revealed: US spy operation that manipulates social media. *The Guardian*. Retrieved from http://www.theguardian.com/technology/2011/mar/17/us-spy-operation-social-networks

Filopovic, J. (2013, October 18). In Maryville, Anonymous must beware risk of vigilantism. *The Guardian*. Retrieved from http://www.theguardian.com/commentisfree/2013/oct/18/maryville-anonymous-beware-risk-vigilantism

FTFY. (2015). FTFY. *Urban Dictionary*. Retrieved from http://www.urbandictionary.com/define.php?term=FTFY

Futrelle, D. (2014, September 8). Zoe Quinn's screenshots of 4Chan's dirty tricks were just the appetizer. Here's the first course of the dinner, directly from the IRC log. *We Hunted the Mammoth*. Retrieved from http://wehuntedthemammoth.com/2014/09/08/zoe-quinns-screenshots-of-4chans-dirty-tricks-were-just-the-appetizer-heres-the-first-course-of-the-dinner-directly-from-the-irc-log/

Gee, J. P. (2003). *What video games have to teach us about learning and literacy*. New York: Palgrave-MacMillan.

Gonciarz, C. (2012, January 10). *U mad? The Internet's guide to idiots*. KG Tofu Media. [Kindle Edition].

Griffith, N. (2016, December 12). How to defeat an autocrat: Flocking behavior. *Nicola Griffith*. Retrieved from https://nicolagriffith.com/2016/12/12/flocking-how-to-defeat-a-predator/

Grimies. (2010). Rules of the Internet. Retrieved from http://rulesoftheinternet.com/

Haque, U. (2015). This is why Twitter is dying (and what you can learn from it). *Medium.com*. Retrieved from https://medium.com/bad-words/why-twitter-s-dying-and-what-you-can-learn-from-it-9ed233e37974

Hardt, M., & Negri, A. (2001). *Empire*. Boston, MA: Harvard University Press.

Hasbro. (2011). Equestria girls promo: Hub extended length. [Commercial]. *YouTube*. Retrieved from https://www.youtube.com/watch?v=pTPqjKk_xCo

Haslam, S. A., & Reicher, S. (2012, November 12). Contesting the nature of conformity: What Milgram and Zimbardo's studies really show. *PLoS Biol, 10*(11). Retrieved from http://journals.plos.org/plosbiology/article?id=10.1371/journal.pbio.1001426

Hathaway, J. (2014). What is GamerGate and why? An explanation for non-geeks. *Gawker*. Retrieved from http://gawker.com/what-is-gamergate-and-why-an-explainer-for-non-geeks-1642909080

Henson, J. (1983–7). *Fraggle Rock*. [Television series]. Toronto, Ontario: Jim Henson Television.

Hern, A. (2015, January 13). Gamergate hits new low with attempts to send SWAT teams to critics. *The Guardian*. Retrieved from http://www.theguardian.com/technology/2015/jan/13/gamergate-hits-new-low-with-attempts-to-send-swat-teams-to-critics

Hess, A. (2014, January 6). Why women aren't welcome on the Internet. *Pacific Standard Magazine*. Retrieved from http://www.psmag.com/health-and-behavior/women-arent-welcome-internet-72170

Hillary, A. (2014, January 25). Autism Speaks are work-stealing, white-texting liars. *Yes, That Too*. Retrieved from http://yesthattoo.blogspot.com/2014/01/autism-speaks-are-work-stealing-white.html#sthash.rRqX-VzQF.dpuf

Hindmann, M. (2008). *The myth of digital democracy*. Princeton, New Jersey: Princeton University Press.

Johansen, A. (2014, August 27). The Creatures (Kootra) got SWAT Raided (SWATTED). #FreeKOOTRA2014. *YouTube*. Retrieved from https://www.youtube.com/watch?v=Nz8yLIOb2pU

Juul, J. (2005). *Half-real: Video Games between real rules and fictional worlds*. Boston, MA: The MIT Press.

Juul, J. (2007). Introduction to game time. In N. Wardrip-Fruin & P. Harrigan. (eds.), *First person: New media as story, performance and game*. Boston, MA: MIT Press.

Kelly, K. (1994). *Out of Control: The rise of neo-biological civilization*. New York: Perseus Books.

Kelly, K. (1998). *New rules for the new economy: 10 radical strategies for a connected world*. New York: Viking Adult.

KnowYourMeme. (2011). Privilege Denying Dude. *KnowYourMeme*. Retrieved from http://knowyourmeme.com/memes/privilege-denying-dude

KnowYourMeme. (2011). Rick Rolling. *Know Your Meme*. Retrieved from http://knowyourmeme.com/memes/rickroll

Kolko, B, Nakamura, L., & Rodman, G. (Eds.). (2000). *Race in cyberspace*. New York: Routledge.

Lastowka, G. (2010, October 26). *Virtual Justice*. New Haven, CT: Yale University Press.

Lay, M. M., Monk, J., & Rosenfelt, D. (Eds). (2001). *Encompassing gender: Integrating area studies, ethnic studies, and women's studies*. New York: The Feminist Press at CUNY.

Lonsway, K., Archambault, J., & Lisak, D. (2009). False reports: Moving beyond the issue to successfully investigate and prosecute non-stranger sexual assault. *NDAA*. Retrieved from http://ndaa.org/pdf/the_voice_vol_3_no_1_2009.pdf

McGlensey, M. (2013, October 13). Hactivist group seeks justice in Maryville. *MS Magazine*. Retrieved from http://msmagazine.com/blog/2013/10/21/hactivist-group-seeks-justice-in-maryville/

McGonigal, J. (2011). *Reality is broken: Why games make us better and how they can change the world*. New York: Penguin Books.

Media Molecule. (2008). *Little Big Planet* [Video Game]. Surrey: United Kingdom: Media Molecule.

Moulton, J. (1983). A paradigm of philosophy: The Adversary Method. Discovering Reality. Springer Netherlands. pp. 149–64. Retrieved from http://link.springer.com/chapter/10.1007%2F0–306–48017–4_9

Nealon, J. (2007). *Foucault beyond Foucault: Power and its intensifications since 1984*. Palo Alto, CA: Stanford University Press.

Network MCI. (1994). No more there [Commercial]. *YouTube*. Retrieved from https://www.youtube.com/watch?v=nJhRPBJPoO0

Niantic. (2013). *Ingress* [Online game]. LibGDX [Engine]. Android, iOS.

Niantic. (2016, July 6). *Pokémon Go* [Online game]. Unity [Engine]. Android, iOS.

Nintendo EAD Group No. 4. (2015). *Super Mario Maker* [Video Game]. Japan: Nintendo.

Nintendo R&D4. (1985). *Super Mario Bros* [Video game]. Japan: Nintendo.

Ohlheiser, A. (2016, November 12). We actually elected a meme as president: How 4Chan celebrated Trump's victory. *Chicago Tribune*. Retrieved fromhttp://www.chicagotribune.com/bluesky/technology/ct-meme-president-4chan-trump-wp-bsi-20161112-story.html

Oppel, R. (2013, March 17). Ohio teenagers guilty in rape that social media brought to light. *New York Times*. Retrieved from http://www.nytimes.com/2013/03/18/us/teenagers-found-guilty-in-rape-in-steubenville-ohio.html?_r=0

Palahniuk, C. (2005, October 17). *Fight Club: A Novel*. New York: W. W. Norton.

Parker, E. (2015). *Now I know who my comrades are: Voices from the Internet Underground* [Kindle Edition]. Sarah Crichton Books.

Parker, T. [Director]. (1998, December 16). Gnomes. *South Park* [Television series]. Braniff Productions.

Parker, T. [Director]. (2005, November 16). Trapped in the Closet. *South Park* [Television series]. Braniff Productions.

PartyVan Wiki. (2011). In *Insurgency Wiki*. Retrieved from https://wiki.partyvan.info/index.php/Main_Page

PartyVan Wiki. (2013). Feminazis. In *Insurgency Wiki*. Retrieved from http://insurg.in/index.php?title=Feminazis

PartyVan/Insurgency Wiki. (2014, July 8). Main page. In *Insurgency Wiki*. Retrieved from http://insurg.in/index.php?title=Main_Page

Penny, S. (2004). Representation, enaction, and the ethics of simulation. In N. Wardrip-Fruin & P. Harrigan (Eds.), *First person: New media as story, performance, and game*. Boston, MA: MIT Press. pp. 73-83.

Phillips, A. (2012, April 10). Five things academics might learn from how the rowdy social justice blogosphere handles fucknecks. *Fembot Collective*. Retrieved from http://fembotcollective.org/blog/2012/04/10/im-not-offended-im-contemptuous-5-things-academics-might-learn-from-how-the-rowdy-social-justice-blogosphere-handles-fucknecks/

Phillips, W. (2015). *This is why we can't have nice things: Mapping the relationship between online trolling and mainstream culture* [Kindle Edition]. Boston, MA: The MIT Press.

Pizza Bomb. (2013). In *Insurgency Wiki*. Retrieved from http://insurg.in/index.php?title=Pizza_bomb

Plato. (1925). *Gorgias*. The Internet Classics Archive. MIT. Retrieved from http://classics.mit.edu/Plato/gorgias.html

Poster, M. (2006). *Information please: Culture and Politics in the age of digital machines*. Durham, NC: Duke University Press Books.

Project Chanology. (2010). In *Encyclopedia Dramatica*. Retrieved from http://www.encylopediadramatica.se

Purchase Order. (2013). In *Insurgency Wiki*. Retrieved from http://insurg.in/index.php?title=Purchase_Order

Quinn, Z. (2013, February 14). *Depression Quest* [Video game]. Retrieved from http://www.depressionquest.com/

Reddit. (2005). *Reddit*. San Francisco, CA: Reddit. Retrieved from http://www.reddit.com

Rick Rolling. (2010). In *Encyclopedia Dramatica*. Retrieved from http://www.encyclopediadramatica.se.

Rockstar Games. (2010). *Red dead redemption* [Video game]. San Diego: Rockstar Games.

Rules of the Internet. (2009). In *Encyclopedia Dramatica*. Retrieved from http://www.encyclopediadramatica.se

Sauter, M. (2014). *The coming swarm: DDOS actions, hacktivism, and civil disobedience* [Kindle Edition]. New York: Bloomsbury Academic.

Schopenhauer, A. (2013). *The Art of controversy* [Kindle Edition]. Indypublish.

Schwartz, M. (2008, August 3). The trolls amongst us. *The New York Times*. Retrieved from http://www.nytimes.com/2008/08/03/magazine/03trolls-t.html?pagewanted=all&_r=0

Selfe, C. (1991). *Technology and literacy in the 21st century: The importance of paying attention*. Carbondale: Southern Illinois University Press.

Selfe, C., & Selfe, R. (1994). The politics of the interface: Power and its exercise in electronic contact zones. *College Composition and Communication*. 45(4). 480–505.

Shirky, C. (2008). *Here comes everybody: The Power of organizing without organizations*. New York: Penguin Books.

Shirky, C. (2010). *Cognitive Surplus: Creativity and generosity in a connected age*. New York: Penguin Press.

Siegel, J. (2013, October 19). The new vigilantes. *The Daily Beast*. Retrieved from http://www.thedailybeast.com/articles/2013/10/19/anonymous-maryville-and-the-new-vigilantism.html

Smith, D. (2008). The 20 year old at the heart of web's most anarchic and influential site. *The Observer*. Retrieved from http://www.theguardian.com/technology/2008/jul/20/internet.google

Socrates. (2015). In *Encyclopedia Dramatica*. Retrieved from https://encyclopediadramatica.se/Socrates

Solow-Niedermann, A. G. (2010). The Power of 140 Characters? #IranElection and Social Movements in Web 2.0. *Intersect: The Stanford Journal of Science, Technology, and Society*, 3(1). Retrieved from http://ojs.stanford.edu/ojs/index.php/intersect/rt/printerFriendly/191/0

Sorkin, A. (1999). *The West Wing* [Television series]. Los Angeles, CA: NBC.

Stone, S. (1995). *The war of desire and technology at the close of the Mechanical Age*. Boston, MA: The MIT Press.

Swarm Canada. (2017). Swarm for change. *Swarm Canada*. Retrieved from https://swarmcanada.wordpress.com/

Sweeney, O. (2013, February 11). *Hackers on steroids: A vigilante journey through the Internet abyss of 4Chan Cyberpaths and Facebook Paedophiles* [Kindle Edition]. Retrieved from Amazon.com

Szulborski, D. (2011, January 19). *This is not a game: A guide to alternate reality gaming* [Kindle Edition]. Retrieved from Amazon.com

The internet is serious business. (2010). In *Encyclopedia Dramatica*. Retrieved from https://encyclopediadramatica.se/Internet_is_serious_business

Toffler, A. (1984). *Future shock*. New York: Bantam.

Turkle, S. (1997). *Life on the Screen: Identity in the Age of the Internet.* New York: Simon and Schuster.

UnholyDemigod. (2012). What pisses you off about Reddit the most? *Reddit.* Retrieved from https://www.reddit.com/r/AskReddit/comments/10mf4r/what_pisses_you_off_about_reddit_the_most/

FTFY. (2015). FTFY. *Urban Dictionary.* Retrieved from http://www.urban-dictionary.com/define.php?term=FTFY

Vitanza, V. (2011, September 27). *Sexual violence in Western thought and writing: Chaste rape.* New York: Palgrave MacMillan.

Walton, D. (1992). *The place of emotion in argument.* State College, PA: Penn State University Press.

Walton, D. (1998). *Ad hominem arguments.* Tuscaloosa, AL: The University of Alabama Press.

Wark, M. (2007, April 30). *Gamer theory.* Boston, MA: Harvard University Press.

Weckerle, A. (2013, February 23). *Civility in the digital age* [Kindle Edition]. Que Publishing.

Whately, R. (1836). *Elements of rhetoric* [PDF file]. London: B. Fellowes.

Williams, M. E. (2015, October 2). 4Chan and the Oregon Shooter: What the suspicious thread says about a horrifying subculture of young male rage. *Salon.* Retrived from http://www.salon.com/2015/10/02/4chan_and_the_oregon_shooter_what_the_suspicious_thread_says_about_a_horrifying_subculture_of_young_male_rage/

ZoeQuinnText. (2013). Zoe Quinn Text.txt. [Text file].

Index

About the Author

Dr. Jill Morris is an Associate Professor of English and Foreign Languages at Frostburg State University in Frostburg, Maryland. She is interested in digital rhetorics, page design, experience architecture, rhetorics of place, and cultural studies. She enjoys riding roller coasters, photography, and playing with her Pomeranians in her spare time. She is currently studying the history of communication in American amusement parks via archival work paired with digital community studies.

Photograph of the author by Gerry Snelson. Used by permission.